NEVER GIVE UP

NEVER GIVE UP

*Break the Connection
Between Stress and Illness*

Alexis Acker-Halbur

NEVER GIVE UP INSTITUTE
St. Paul, Minnesota

Alex is available for speaking engagements, book discussions, and class facilitation. Contact her via e-mail at nevergiveupinstitute@gmail.com.

Never Give Up: Break the Connection Between Stress and Illness
Copyright © 2014 by Alexis Acker-Halbur

NEVER GIVE UP INSTITUTE
St. Paul, Minnesota

For information about NEVER GIVE UP INSTITUTE programs, visit nevergiveupinstitute.org.

All rights reserved. No part of this book may be reproduced, stored in or introduced into a retrieval system, or transmitted, in any form or by any means (electronic, mechanical, photocopying, recording or otherwise), without the prior permission of the copyright holder.

Cover design and illustrations: Stacy Drudesign
Cover photo: iStockphoto.com-Alex7021

To order this book in print or e-book format, visit Amazon.com.

ISBN: 978-1-4949-8424-3

Library of Congress Control Number: 2014906797

Printed in the United States of America

This book does not attempt to diagnose or treat any illness. The information presented is not intended to replace the advice of health care professionals.

*To all the survivors and thrivers I know,
have worked with, and cherish:*

*May you feel love and joy
as you find meaning in your lives.
You are my heroes.*

Contents

Foreword xiii
Acknowledgments xv

Introduction 1

1
Beginning Your Journey to Better Health and Well-Being

1 CAUTION: Stress Is Extremely Dangerous 5
   Activity 1: Relieve Stress with Music 11

2 The Nasty and Nurturing Sides of Anger 12
   Activity 2: Release Unhealthy Anger 19

3 The Mind-Body-Spirit Connection in Healing 20
   Activity 3: Explore the Mind-Body-Spirit Connection 28

2
Stopping Violence and Trauma from Affecting Your Health

4 The Truth About Childhood Sexual Abuse 31
   Activity 4: Release Emotions Through Writing 46

5 Healing from Rape 47
   Activity 5: Reflect on *The Scream* by Edvard Munch 54

6 The Nightmare of Sexual Exploitation 55
   Activity 6: Draw the Connection Between Stress/Trauma and Illness 64

3
Strengthening Your Immune System After Injury and Illness

7 Osteoarthritis Defense 67
   Activity 7: Take Steps to Improve Your Attitude and Strength 73

8 Auto Accident Survival 74
   Activity 8: Put Premium Fuel in Your Body 81

9 Illness as Trauma 82
   Activity 9: Heal Your Heart Quadrants 89

10   Diabetes: It's Not Just About Sugar   91
     Activity 10: Make Healthy Choices at the Salad Bar   97

11   Sleep Apnea: When You Can't Breathe When You Sleep   98
     Activity 11: Change Your Batteries for Better Sleep   105

12   Cancer: A Life Changer   107
     Activity 12: Reflect on Your Friendships   123

4
Living with Your New Changes

13   Your New Normal   127
     Activity 13: Reflect on Your New Normal   132

14   Setbacks in Healing   133
     Activity 14: Cope with Setbacks   139

5
Understanding Death—
Yours and Your Loved Ones'

15   Death as a New Beginning   143
     Activity 15: Choose 10 Meaningful Things to Do Before You Die   148

16   Death by Suicide   149
     Activity 16: Create Your Success Chart   153

17	How to Talk with Your Dying Loved Ones 156
	Activity 17: Plan Your End-of-Life Celebration 160

6

Healing, Surviving, and Thriving

18	How You Can Survive and Thrive 165
	Activity 18: Name Your Reasons for Fighting and Overcoming Adversity 166
19	Strength and Healing 167
	Activity 19: Strengthen Your Memory 170
20	The Healing Power of Gratitude 171
	Activity 20: Show Gratitude 175
21	Angels to the Rescue 176
	Activity 21: Develop Resiliency 181
22	I Believe in Hope 183
	Activity 22: Write Your Bucket List of Hope 186
23	Self-Inspiration to Get You Going 187
	Activity 23: Create Your Inspiration Wall 191
24	Don't Forget Forgiveness 192
	Activity 24: Practice Forgiveness and Letting Go 197
25	Life Passion 198
	Activity 25: Finish the Sentence "I Love Myself Because…" 200

7
Putting Your New Life Together

26 What It All Means 203
    Activity 26: Turn Old Thoughts into New Thoughts 205

27 What I Learned from Cancer 206

8
Fine-Tuning Your Tools

28 Your Most Valuable Tools 211

Exercises

1   Life Stress Test 212
2   When I . . . 214
3   Things I Like to Do List 217
4   Your Tools 218

Resources 221
Sources Cited 223

Foreword

This book is about Hope with a capital H. I chose the capital H because it adds a spiritual dimension to the concept of hope, placing it on an infinite continuum—unwavering, eternal, and with unlimited possibilities, including the miraculous. This expanded concept of Hope, which is reflected within these pages, creates an unshakeable foundation under the main theme: never give up—because every possibility exists at every moment, including the miraculous, no matter how dismal the current situation or news may be.

Alex Acker-Halbur does a superb job of making the contents of her book come alive. Unlike many authors who do a good job of leading the reader along a path toward the goal they are promoting, Alex steps right out of these pages, takes your hand, and walks the journey with you toward healing. She can do it because she has walked that journey herself—many times—with the same successful result, and she is not afraid to do it again.

I get to work alongside Alex, so I know that she means—and personifies—every word she speaks in her classes and writes in this book. I am a witness to her many success stories.

Never Give Up is essential for anyone who has struggled against adversity, faced devastating circumstances, including life-threatening illness, and has lost hope in ever achieving wellness. If you are in this group, you are exactly the person this book was written for, and you are exactly the person this healer is eager to work with.

—Paul L. Berry, PhD, Licensed Clinical Psychologist
Well Within, a nonprofit
holistic wellness resource center

Acknowledgments

It's with immense gratitude that I acknowledge the following individuals who have helped me write this book: my wife, Rita L. Acker-Halbur; my special associate, Dr. Paul Berry; my therapists throughout the years; my incredible friends Shelly Medernach, Kate Huebsch, Tammy Hilliard, Sandy Hyde, and Peg DuBois†; my wise mentors Mary Burke, Robyn Calmenson†, and Mary O'Keefe. I also want to acknowledge and thank my expert physicians and surgeons at Regions Hospital Cancer Care Center and Abbott-Northwestern Hospital and my wonderful staff and friends at Well Within and Pathways Minneapolis.

I could not have put this book together without the amazing work of these publishing professionals: Stacy Drude Rose, Barbara Drewlo, Angie Schneeman, and Ann Delgehausen, Beth Wright, and Zan Ceeley of Trio Bookworks.

Blessings from my heart and love to you all.

Introduction

Surviving is important. Thriving is elegant.
—**Maya Angelou**

Our world is filled with obstacles that prevent us from living a healthy, meaningful life. Past experiences of stress, trauma, and loss make us sick without our knowing. We seek medical professionals to tell us what's wrong, or at least give us pills to eradicate our suffering. Our out-of-pocket medical expenses are skyrocketing. What can you do to reduce illness and make yourself healthier?

You can start with yourself!

Scientific research shows that we can improve the quality of our lives by focusing on our mind, body, and spirit. This vital connection is a paradigm shift in how we view stress and illness.

How do I know this? *Never Give Up* is my true story of survival.

I was in a hospital bed, diagnosed with stage 4 colon cancer, and fighting for my life—not once but twice. I suddenly saw the connection on how stress, trauma, and loss made me so sick. I knew at that moment I needed to survive and find ways to help myself physically, emotionally, and spiritually cope with my experiences. I am not a medical professional, but I am a professional patient. As someone who has weathered many illnesses and losses, I wrote this book to help me understand and expand my knowledge of stress-related illnesses.

If you're dealing with a history of stress or abuse, a diagnosis of a chronic or life-threatening illness, or a major loss or trauma in your life, this book is for you. It will help you learn how illness and trauma affect you and provides tools and activities you can use to improve the quality of your life. All the tools mentioned in this book are interchangeable, and you can use them for coping with different types of trauma.

Please note: Some of my stories are disturbing. It is not my intention to retrigger your nightmares. The first three chapters, while describing some of the traumas I have survived, provide a solid foundation on the nature of healing. You'll learn about my experiences and how I live my life with purpose, meaning, and a sense of well-being. The twenty-six activities that come at the end of the main chapters are meant to help you develop your coping skills and gain insight into your strengths. The four exercises at the end of the book will help you identify the tools that will work best for you. I've also included a list of resources you can use to find more information on specific topics.

Finally, as you learn to cope with your personal challenges in life, and as you incorporate the tools and insights from this book, please remember: *Never give up!*

NEVER GIVE UP

1

Beginning Your Journey to Better Health and Well-Being

CAUTION:
Stress Is Extremely Dangerous

*Stress is when you wake up screaming
and realize you haven't fallen asleep yet.*
—Unknown

One night during my senior year in college, I was about to head out the door to attend class. The phone rang; it was Mom telling me she'd been diagnosed with breast cancer. Fear and anxiety seized my throat and froze my heart. Mom told me not to worry because on Tuesday she was having surgery to remove her breasts. I promised her I'd come home on the weekend to see her. I went to class but couldn't stop thinking about her. On the way home to my apartment that night I repeatedly screamed, "IT'S NOT FAIR!" I could see my breath in the chilly night.

I couldn't find a ride to my parents' house that weekend and fretted about what was happening to Mom. Then a freezing snowstorm began, ultimately closing highways from the university to home. I was distraught. The fear that Mom would die before I could see her again hung around my neck like a noose. My greatest fear—losing my mom—was now happening for real. I cried buckets of tears for two weeks until I could see Mom again. She had a total mastectomy and started the healing process. In addition to the surgery, she had to go through radiation and chemotherapy. I prayed daily for her recovery from breast cancer, and after five years, Mom was in remission.

Thirty-three years later, I realized I still carried the stress of Mom's cancer. My countless medical records were proof.

Our bodies are created to handle acute stress—a very short-term type of stress such as being five to ten minutes late for an appointment. Thousands of studies now focus on chronic stress—the type of stress that seems inescapable and endless, like caring for a critically ill parent or child.

In most chronic stress situations, something happens repeatedly, leaving you with no sense of control. It could be a series of surgeries, illnesses, or abnormally high tension. These all affect your health in negative ways. When you can't get your mind and body to relax, you feel depleted and fatigued. Studies show that stress can be a contributing factor to virtually all major illnesses since it can lower immunity. This is important to know because chronic stress can desensitize the immune system's response to infections and can weaken our response to immunizations. Those of us under chronic stress show low white blood cell counts, making us more prone to colds. Researchers say that stress actually increases cold symptoms.

In retrospect, I finally see the big picture on how stress has affected the quality of my life. Though I tried not to, I stressed over everything in my life. I was a stress-o-matic.

According to the American Academy of Family Physicians, two-thirds of all office visits to family doctors are due to stress-related symptoms. *Business Insider* writer Ashley Lutz provides some other examples:

- Your body can't tell the difference between a big stress and a small one. Stressing over traffic every day could have the same negative impact on your health as a divorce.
- A British study shows that the more people check their smart phones, the more stressed they become.
- Using email also has detrimental effects. Researchers found that a group of workers who were cut off from office email use for five days experienced more natural, variable heart rate.
- Long-term stress can disrupt nearly all of the body's processes and increase the risk of developing health problems.
- Increased stress leads to increased inflammation of the body, meaning you're more susceptible to immune disorders.

These points are just some of the scientific evidence on how stress dangerously affects our health. Yet there is another stress monster that can make you sick. I want to enlighten you on the effects of secondhand stress.

Have you been in a checkout lane at the grocery store feeling irritated? A migraine is starting, your hands are trembling, and you feel nauseous. "What's happening to me?" you ask yourself, knowing you didn't feel this way fifteen minutes ago. Then you notice a mother with two children in front of you. Mom seems unaware that her small children are reaching over and grabbing unpaid-for items on the nearby shelf. They open two candy bars, take a bite, and then put the bars back on the shelf. Mom raises her voice at the clerk, and you notice your shoulders tensing. You want to scream. You want nothing more than to run away. "What's happening to me?" you wonder again.

This is known as "secondhand stress" (tension we pick up from others) and is highly contagious. New research finds that if you are near someone who is experiencing stress, you may become a carrier and pass stress on to others. Stress travels in social networks. Being aware of how tense you're becoming can lead to immediate action. Leave the situation, and go sit in your car in the parking lot. Take a deep breath, and then slowly exhale the air from your lungs. This may take three or four breaths before you can feel the tension leave your body.

Tools to Cope with Stress

Here are some tools to help relieve stress and bring your body into balance before you get sick.

1. Eat right. Make sure you eat enough healthy foods. Sometimes you may indulge in junk food when you're feeling sad, and although a little bit of this is okay, too much can be bad for your health.

2. Sleep. Stress often disrupts sleep patterns. Under severe stress, you may want to sleep constantly, or you may find it difficult to sleep because of worry about what the future holds. Research suggests that sleep is important in helping us process information and function effectively. So if possible, try to get at least seven to eight hours of sleep per night.

3. Get regular exercise. Research suggests that physical exercise can help you deal with stress, and there is evidence that exercise can affect your brain functioning.

4. Find emotional support. Seek out positive people who will encourage your coping efforts and who remind you that stress is a normal feeling you can overcome.

5. Take time for yourself. Taking time out for yourself to do something enjoyable will help relieve stress and help keep your spirits

up. This might include hobbies such as knitting, gardening, cooking, sports, art, or other fun activities. Any activity that you enjoy, such as listening to music, reading, or watching a favorite television program, can be beneficial. It helps to establish a routine in which you engage in your own enjoyment every day, even if it is only for five to ten minutes.

6. Try to maintain a positive attitude. How we think about things affects how well we cope with the situation. One thing that can help you maintain a positive attitude is remembering that it is natural to be sad or angry at times, and it is important not to judge your feelings. If you have a spiritual practice, seeking solace in your religious community or practices such as prayer or meditation can be helpful.

7. Explore Higher Brain Living. I've always found meditation and massage to be great ways to help me relieve my stress, but I'm always looking for new treatments to stay healthy. In 2011, my friend Becky and I discovered Higher Brain Living (HBL) at an informational session presented by Dr. Michael Cotton, developer of the Higher Brain Living Technique. Becky decided to be trained in HBL. Fourteen months later, she was a certified HBL facilitator, and I began to receive HBL treatments from her.

An HBL session involves a gentle-touch technique that creates "a surge of energy from your primal fear-based lower brain into your prefrontal cortex, the seat of the higher brain, where your potential lives." The technique enables "a feedback mechanism that brings life-sustaining oxygen and increased metabolism into the Higher Brain," releasing stress and rejuvenating every cell in the body.

My goal is to eliminate the anxiety, worry, and stress I feel and replace it with abundance, confidence, and joy. My sessions are a way to attain this goal. There are three tiers of HBL. Tier 1 energizes my higher brain and body where stress is released, and I experience more clarity and lightness. Tier 2 continues to energize my prefrontal cortex, leading to more empowerment, and allows me to locate the "hot spots" in my life that are holding me back from attaining my dreams. Tier 3 creates deeper connections and new patterns in my higher brain so that I can live a life with more depth and purpose. I find HBL to be a great source of help for my healing.

ACTIVITY 1

Relieve Stress with Music

SUPPLIES: radio, stereo, CDs, or mp3 player

Listening to music is a great mood enhancer and stress reliever. It can calm you down or perk you up. What you listen to affects you!

An elderly man was hospitalized because of high blood pressure and stress. A friend of mine came into his room, sat in a chair next to him, and began to sing soothing songs. While he listened to her music, the monitor showed that his blood pressure went down.

You can categorize your music in your daily life for relaxation, to gain energy when feeling drained, or to help you deal with emotional and physical stress. Sing and dance your way to better health!

What are your favorite "happy" songs?
....

What songs do you listen to when you exercise?
....

What type of songs help you to relax?
....

Are there song lyrics that live in your heart and mind?
....

Which songs build your self-confidence?
....

What song would you like to sing to your body?
....

The Nasty and Nurturing Sides of Anger

Anger is a normal emotion. There are two sides of anger, however: the nasty side of anger, which lowers your ability to fight off infections, and the nurturing side of anger, which strengthens your immune system by releasing stress and increasing your white blood cells. When we learn to release anger through appropriate means, we can safely cope with it. Indeed, healthy ways of expressing anger can prevent you from getting sick.

Anger-generating thoughts can be hurtful and disruptive. Just look at the driver in the car next to you on a crowded freeway. Is he/she screaming, using profanity, and/or making physical gestures? If road rage is this strong, can you imagine what might be going on in this person's home or office? In this chapter, you'll learn how to reduce the side effects of anger in ways that fortify your health.

The Unhealthy Side of Anger

As a child, I never learned how to express anger in a nurturing way. The only one in the family allowed to get angry was my dad, and from how he handled his anger, I learned early in my life that anger was a very bad thing.

When my dad got angry, he swore, he slammed things, he hit, and he threw Sunday lunches down the drain. His face would turn purple, and the veins would stick out of his face. He'd clench his hands to the point where his arms would shake. He would look as if he were ready to explode—and he often did.

It didn't matter what Dad was angry about. It could've been that his football team lost or the tile in the bathroom wasn't his preferred shade of pink. It didn't matter. He'd just blow. You can imagine how scary this was for me. I never knew when he'd get angry, but when he did, I'd hide. It was safer than getting in his way, since he might hit me.

In Chapter 3, I'll discuss how responses to threats can be fight, flight, or freeze. Coming face to face with Dad when he was angry, I'd freeze. To see the anger in his eyes was enough to scare me to the core of my existence.

When my mother was angry, she'd yell or withdraw (aka the silent treatment). This is another nasty side of anger.

As a child, I didn't want to be like my dad when he got angry—but I was. The few times I exploded and smashed things, I was punished, so I learned very quickly to keep my anger stuffed inside me. I followed my mother with the silent treatment—I emotionally and physically withdrew. Becoming silent seemed to be the perfect thing to do when I felt angry.

You can imagine what all that stored-up energy can do to your body if not released. My body rebelled, and I got sick. I suffered from severe migraines and developed high blood pressure. Still I would not express my anger. Well into my forties, I began to realize how harmful this was to me emotionally and physically. I worked with therapists on how I could constructively express my anger, but it was difficult, though not impossible.

If I got angry and I made someone cry, I felt like a loser. I saw my dad in my anger and my behavior, and that made me sulk. My anger started turning into depression. The angrier I got, the more depressed I became. I realized I had to do something about expressing my anger and releasing old incidents. If I didn't, I was bound to keep getting sick.

The Healthy Side of Anger

Then along came my friend Joni. When Joni got angry, she would stick out both of her middle fingers and scream, "Fuck you!" At first, her anger frightened me, and I drew away from her, but then I noticed something: making the gesture and screaming out the words actually seemed to help her. I went home and tried it. (Of course, I was alone at the time.) Slowly I began to see that doing this really made a difference for me. I felt better. After several weeks, I decided that I didn't need the middle finger gestures. I just needed to scream, "Fuck you!"

When cancer came along, I started talking to the cancer. I'd end every conversation with "Fuck you, cancer!" (I generally find the "F" word offensive, but in moments of rage, I've found it effectively relieves my tension.)

It also helped me to hear my friends express their anger at the cancer. Right after I heard that cancer was in my liver the second time, I wrote the following on my CaringBridge website:

> *Thursday, March 20, 2008*
>   *Hello out there:*
>   *Before the narcotics kick in and I'm reduced to a limp body on the carpet, I thought I'd let you know what we found out at today's liver biopsy.*
>   *I have cancer—again.*

It seems ironic that for two years in a row—on the same day—I find out that I have cancer. Apparently, as my liver was growing back, so did the cancer cells.

Yes, I'm angry but relieved we finally know what's going on with my liver. I'm not scared, just disappointed that my body was unable to prevent more growth. Like I said last year, the war isn't over but I'm going to win this battle. Luckily, I have all of you in my troop—that's F-Troop to you cancer!

Thanks for keeping me in your prayers. Of the three doctors I consulted, one doctor wanted to take a "wait and see" approach, but your prayers shed light on what has to be done immediately. Thank you.

Love, Alex

Six days later, I received the following entry from my friend Jacky:

Wednesday, March 26, 2008

Dear Alex,

Oh honey, hang in there...

Come on let's kick some fuckin' ass!!!!!!!!!!!

I hate the cancer that's invading your body. I hate it, I hate it, I hate it!

Feel our strength Alex; we are beside you holding you up. You can fight this. You have all this energy running through you from your family and friends. We are here in strength, faith, and hope. Even if you need to rest...

Love you, Jacky

I love this message because it was exactly how I felt. I was proud of myself because I began to express my anger about the new diagnosis. I didn't hide from my anger. The response I got from friends and family was consistent: "It's about time you showed your anger."

Gee, I didn't think anyone had noticed. But my friends and family had. It was like a Discovery Channel episode: "Alex Voices Her Anger and Doesn't Get Sick." (I believe my dad had several heart attacks during anger episodes.)

I've also learned that I need to do something physical with my anger. I do yard work or clean when I'm angry. It has to be something that makes me sweat. I view the perspiration as the anger being released from my body. Then when I'm done, I take a shower. I feel good inside and out, and my anger is neutralized.

I now see anger as a good thing rather than a bad thing. There are destructive ways to express anger, but I learned what expressions were useful to me and not harmful to someone else.

In "Is Suppressed Anger Making You Sick?" Courtney Prosser, an occupational therapist, counselor, wellness coach, and author, poignantly describes managing anger:

> In its purest form, anger is concentrated balls of fire that bubble up from our depths. These balls of fire are our deepest passions, our life force, our fuel for change and one of the most useful superpowers available to us in life!
>
> Suppress your fire and you mute your power as a human being. You may also be making yourself unwell and unhappy. . . .
>
> Over the years, through trial and error and making lots of so-called mistakes along the way, I've slowly learned to love my fire.

The image of fire is a great way to visualize anger. I've built cooking fires in fireplaces and at campsites, so I know how quickly fire spreads among dry wood, leaves, and twigs. Anger can either hurt you or warm you. Destructive anger is much like a wild, uncontrolled fire—it burns everything in its path. Healthy anger is a source of comfort and warmth. You can control the anger and express it in many healing ways.

If no one's ever told you that expressing your anger is healthy and the right thing to do, then take my advice: get help and get angry! Remember that anger is a normal feeling. Unhealthy anger can make you sick by weakening your immune system. Don't let anger play havoc with your body and mind. Therapists and counselors who specialize in anger management can help you express anger in appropriate ways.

Tools to Express Anger in Healthy Ways

Below are some tools I've found helpful in trying to express anger without harming myself or others.

1. Be aware of your anger. For many of us, anger comes on suddenly. You negatively react to an issue, and your anger rises to the surface. Once lit, your anger spreads through your body like a wildfire. Uncontrolled anger can affect your relationships and your health, so the healthiest thing to do is to stop yourself before you react. Take several deep breaths. Acknowledge the anger, and continue to breathe.

2. Remember that your anger may be the tip of the iceberg. Below the surface may be other emotions, like hurt, resentment, frustration, fear, sadness, and depression. It's important to identify these feelings so that you can choose a healthy way to express them.

3. Acknowledge that expressing anger is under your control. You have the choice to express it in a healthy or harmful way. When you're angry, do you criticize or blame others? Do you use sarcasm? Do you throw or break things? Do you hurt yourself or others? If you answered yes to any of these questions, you should realize there

are better ways of expressing your anger. Take the time to understand if fear is driving your response. Take several deep breaths and let yourself exhale completely. Do this until you feel calmer.

4. Know your anger triggers. Does traffic, weather, or disappointment irritate you? Do you become angry when you're tired? List your personal triggers and your typical responses to remind your mind, body, and spirit to express your anger in healing ways.

5. Seek professional help. When your response to anger is unhealthy, it may be time to seek outside help. If your anger seems out of control, causes you to do things you regret, or hurts those around you, find professional support. Take an anger management class, or find a counselor. You're not alone in seeking professional assistance. Many of us do.

ACTIVITY 2

Release Unhealthy Anger

SUPPLIES: water balloons, rocks, car, golf club and balls, tennis balls, or bat and softball

We all handle anger differently. Some of us get upset quickly and take our feelings out on anyone nearby. This behavior over time can strain relationships and cause stress for everyone involved. You can learn to find safe ways to release your anger so it doesn't build up and affect your relationships. Any physical activity (running, walking, playing a sport) can be part of dealing with anger. You can also try one or more of these ideas:

Fill balloons with water and throw them at concrete buildings (just stay away from windows or anything breakable) or granite boulders. Don't forget to pick up the balloon debris afterward.

Sit in your car in an empty parking lot or somewhere away from traffic or crowds. Scream your anger out the window, if no one is around. Otherwise, keep the windows closed and scream away.

- Throw a softball into the ballpark fence or use a bat and hit balls as far as you can.
- Throw a tennis ball against the garage or a concrete wall.
- Go to a driving range and hit golf balls.
- Stand near a lake or creek and throw rocks in the water.
- Pound your fist into a pillow or a pile of blankets.

The Mind-Body-Spirit Connection in Healing

For much of my life I was scared and angry. I didn't trust anyone, and my defense was being passive-aggressive. When I finally found a therapist I could trust, I began my education on the interrelationship of mind, body, and spirit. At first I thought this was just some New Age woo-woo, but now I realize that it's a formula for transformation. If something is bothering you emotionally, you can bet that somewhere in your body, a muscle, organ, cell, or nerve is being harmed, and so is your spirit.

There is a wealth of research on the mind-body-spirit connection. Let's start by looking at nature for an example of homeostasis, or the tendency in humans and in nature to maintain an inner stability—what might also be called "balance."

Look at a majestic oak or towering pine tree. Isn't it amazing that—considering its size and weight—it doesn't just topple over? If you dug into the earth, you'd find out why. The underground root system mirrors the length of the tree you see aboveground. The tree and its root system are perfectly balanced.

Surviving trauma without becoming sick is a matter of balance. In their article "The Mind-Body Interaction in Disease," Esther M.

Sternberg and Philip W. Gold explain how the human stress response system is triggered in threatening situations. Our immune system is similarly triggered; it reacts to pathogens and foreign molecules. These responses are the body's way to maintain balance. To put it simply, your brain (mind) and your immune system (body) are constantly signaling each other along cell, nerve, and muscular pathways.

There are still a lot of health professionals who question the validity of the mind-body connection. Lucky for us, the research being done by the National Institutes of Health is proving that, indeed, your state of mind influences your health.

Fight, Flight, or Freeze

Many studies concentrate on the consequences of child sexual abuse on our health. What they are finding is the effects of child sexual abuse often includes poorer health, with more physical symptoms, more physician-coded medical diagnoses, and twice the emergency room visits compared to those who never experience sexual abuse as a child.

Unfortunately, for victims of violence, many deal with trauma by consuming alcohol, drugs, or food that results in addictions or depression and suicidal thoughts. Human nature drives us to survive the trauma—commonly referred to as the "fight-or-flight response."

Since the fight-or-flight response is so important to our survival, let's take a moment to define it. First of all, it now is commonly referred to as the fight, flight, or freeze response, as James Porter explains in his article, "Fight, Flight or Freeze Response to Stress":

> Stress experts around the world are adding the word freeze to the name in deference to the fact that instead of fighting or fleeing, sometimes we tend to freeze (like a

deer in the headlights) in traumatic situations. The fight or flight response (in its original form) is about survival. It's about hope. We activate it when we believe there's a chance we can outrun or outfight our attackers. The freeze response, however, gets activated when there's no hope.

For human beings, the freeze response can occur when we're terrified and feel like there is no chance for our survival or no chance for escape. It happens in car accidents, to rape victims, and to people who are robbed at gunpoint. Sometimes they pass out, freeze or mentally remove themselves from their bodies, and don't feel the pain of the attack, and sometimes have no (explicit) memory of it afterwards.

That's why the fight or flight response is now called the fight, flight or freeze response. Because sometimes, when the odds are overwhelming we neither fight nor flee but simply freeze.

Our fight, flight, or freeze response evolved as a survival mechanism to react quickly to life-threatening situations. As an abused child, I knew I couldn't fight my perpetrator (because he was bigger than me), I couldn't take flight (because I knew the abuse would be worse when he caught me), but I could freeze (which my body did on many occasions).

Do you remember the times your body went into the fight, flight, or freeze response? Does one reaction occur more than the others, or does your response change in different circumstances? Does your response result in a harmful or healthy resolution? The body can also overreact to stressors that are not life-threatening, such as traffic jams, work pressures, and family difficulties. Answering these questions will help you teach yourself how to react in positive ways.

In "Consequences of Child Sexual Abuse in a Woman's Life" Pam Hyatt and Caroline White describe how children frequently respond to abuse:

> The trauma of child sexual abuse can grow in silence like a malignant tumor. It often brands its victim and interrupts the natural development flow of childhood. It can send a child's body reeling in fight-flight-freeze mode. When there is no escape, the body often succumbs to the abuse and the mind escapes—severing itself from the only home it has ever known, determined to keep from being exposed to a society that prefers silence over truth.

The fight, flight, or freeze response is one sign that our minds, bodies, and spirits are so intricately connected that we can't affect one without affecting the others.

So where does the spirit come in?

The word "spirit" is much easier to define by what it's not than what it is. The word is often associated with organized religion, but I've found in my life that it goes far beyond that. Your spirit is like the gas needed to run your car. The chassis (body) of the car and the engine (mind) won't work unless the car has gas (spirit).

Your spirit—your raw life force energy—is what gets you up and makes you go. Your spirit is an essential part of our human nature, and without it we would cease to exist. Many people use their raw life force energy to better themselves. This includes living in nature, concentrating on their strengths rather than their weaknesses, praying or meditating, volunteering or raising money for a cause, or loving themselves.

What kind of fuel (energy) do you put in your car (body)? Do you give your body good food, your mind a time to rest, and your

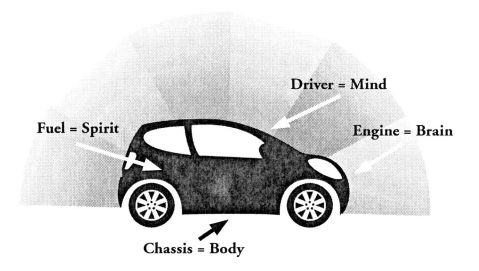

spirit rejuvenating exercises? If not, it is time to change some habits that may not be giving you the energy you need.

You know you're in your spirit mode when you feel a sense of joy, marvel, awe, contentment, exhilaration, peacefulness, pleasure, and happiness. You can define your own spirit.

So when you think of spirit, think of it as life force energy for your mind and body.

What happens when your car runs out of fuel or gets bad gas? It stops. The same thing applies to your body and mind. Therefore, it's important that you keep your spirit full. You can always tell when you're low on spirit. You usually look depressed (because you are). You don't smile or laugh (because you can't). Life feels like a burden rather than a gift. You don't feel well, yet your symptoms are vague.

For example, for many people who love to run, running is not just a physical hobby but also a spiritual one. While moving, runners often experience a sense of calmness, joy, and vitality (energy).

If they stop running for several days, however, they experience the opposite. They've run out of gas.

That's why the mind-body-spirit connection is so important. If any of these run low, the others are affected. They must remain balanced at all times—which is far easier to say than to do.

When trauma hits, it disrupts the balance of the mind, body, and spirit. Sometimes the mind may take the trauma the hardest. A mental imbalance results, and depression, denial, anger, or grief may appear. If the body takes the hit, illness or disease may result. If the spirit takes the hit, you may find your "will to live" draining. Most likely, trauma—no matter what kind—affects all three at once. That's why trauma is so deadly.

Let's also look at the mind and the body. I used to think that the mind is the brain, but I found that this is incorrect. Our brains are physical objects that can be x-rayed and seen with the eyes. Surgeons can touch the brain. Unlike the brain, the mind is not a physical object. We can't see the mind—it's simply part of the body. Our body and mind are different. In Buddhist scriptures, our body is compared to a guesthouse and our mind a guest dwelling within it. When we die, our mind leaves our body and goes to the next life, just like a guest leaves a guesthouse and goes somewhere else.

Our mind is not our brain. The mind functions to perceive and understand objects. Because the mind is formless, you can't hurt it with physical objects. You can, however, injure your mind with negative ideas and thoughts.

How Our Minds Influence Our Health

I'm so amazed at what the mind can do and how it helped me to survive. I frequently read stories about people who've overcome extremely difficult circumstances. Even the people I meet have incredible stories of survival—such as a friend of mine who is going through chemotherapy. When a severe storm raged through the Twin Cities, lightning struck my friend's house. It burned to the ground and destroyed her and her husband's two cars. On her Facebook page, she said something amazing, "We got our two cats safely out of the house. We weren't hurt."

Survivors are people (and animals, too) who can stay alive despite all odds. Survival is a state of mind. If you have the ability to deal with the stress and fear that accompany emergencies, you survive. Survival is the brain's best survival tool. You don't have to be physically strong, but you do have to rely on your natural instincts.

Our minds have the power to will the body to do extraordinary feats. Real life experiences consistently show that our will alone is the major reason for surviving emergencies. Survival is impossible without the will to live. As survivalist and author Chris Conway writes, "What affects you mentally affects you physically. If you think that you can't survive, then you won't try to survive. A commitment or goal to live, refusal to give up, and positive mental attitude greatly increase chances for survival."

So why can't we survive stress, trauma, and loss without becoming ill? It's possible you never were trained, or you ignore your natural instincts. You have to work on your survival every day. I enhance my survival to make me a thriver. Being a survivor is a blessing. Being a thriver means it's now time to live beyond survival and create a new insight and strategy to cope with trauma and chronic stress without getting ill.

Looking back at the traumatic events in my life, I can clearly see how I survived—and how you can survive, too. Your mind, body, and spirit are powerful tools. Together they can prepare us for anything and keep us healthy.

As you read about my sets of survival tools throughout *Never Give Up*, consider your own tool kit. Use them to craft a more worthwhile and illness-free life.

The following activity helps you think of your mind, body, and spirit separately. Use your imagination and create a balanced connection to heal each part.

ACTIVITY 3

Explore the Mind-Body-Spirit Connection

SUPPLIES: pencils (plain or colored) or pens

Select one word to represent your mind. Write the word next to the image below labeled "Mind." Be as creative as you like. Now, select one word that represents your body, and write it next to the image labeled "Body." Finally, select a word to represent your spirit, and write it next to the "Spirit" image below.

Reflect on these questions by yourself or with friends:

➤ Why did you pick a particular word?

➤ What does that word mean to you?

➤ How does that word make you feel?

➤ What are the connections between the words?

MIND   BODY   SPIRIT

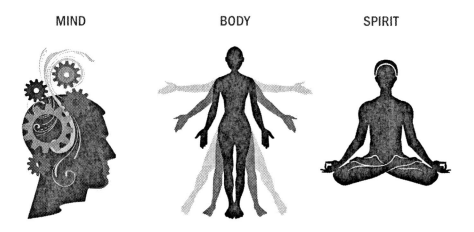

Never Give Up

2

Stopping Violence and Trauma from Affecting Your Health

The Truth About Childhood Sexual Abuse

I never met the wise and creative Karly Wahlin. Karly lived with Rett syndrome for twenty-seven years. She wrote "Healing," a poem about child abuse. I am grateful to Lois Swope, Karly's mom, for allowing me to include it here.

> Time gives our thoughts a place in our hearts
> Places that need healing from broken moments
> To look for understanding,
> for kind responses
> It doesn't always happen
>
> We look for peace and then realize
> it comes from allowing other broken hearts
> a different way to heal
> We see there is more than one way to
> look at the same moment in time

> We let our deepest thoughts be known by God
> and love those in front of us
> who may not feel the same way

Children are suffering from a not-so-hidden-anymore epidemic of child abuse and neglect. Every year 3.3 million reports of child abuse are made in the United States involving 6 million children. According to the U.S. Department of Health and Human Services, Administration for Children and Families Bureau, the United States has the worst record of the industrialized nations—losing five children every day to abuse-related deaths.

Statistics on child abuse and maltreatment are disturbing, but I'm appalled when I think of the individuals behind the numbers. Their lives are so damaged that they can never heal—or so once I believed. Now I know abuse victims can heal and enhance their quality of life. It's an individual choice—a tough choice—that can heal the mind, body, and spirit.

Once Upon a Time . . .

My father started sexually, physically, and emotionally abusing me when I was four years old.

Like many abusive men, my father, too, is a statistic. When he was a young boy, a man who lived in his neighborhood sexually abused him. The trauma to my father—and to me—led us to the same side effects of low self-image, a lack of confidence, and the need for attention. Unfortunately, my father took his abuse and continued the ugly cycle that befalls many (but not all) child victims. We must stop this horrendous cycle!

My father never learned how to survive his early childhood trauma. When he was growing up, in his father's bar, alcohol became a tool for hiding his pain and dark memories. His overuse of alcohol created a strong yet false self-image. He was powerful as long as he had his bottle of whiskey in one hand and a shot glass in the other. My father drank because he hurt and because he was abused. He drank to express his anger, and he learned that anger was power.

My father learned he could control people with his anger.

Child abuse is an issue of power—and of money. The yearly economic impact of child abuse is estimated in the billions. However, I have no statistics to tell you how much it cost me to lose my self-esteem and self-confidence, no cost figures for the guilt and shame I felt, no dollars attributed to the secret I had to keep, and no financial reports on what it cost for the therapy I received for my "side effects."

How much did it cost my father to degrade and frighten me? What did it cost him to wipe his semen on me and then tell me to go wash up because I was dirty—because I smelled bad? What did it cost me when he made me touch him while I stood in my nightgown unable to stop the urine flowing down my legs? How much did it cost me? How much did I lose?

I lost everything—my mind, body, and spirit!

I was too young to understand the atrocities of child sexual abuse. As I grew older, I accepted the anger and hatred I saw in my father's eyes while he sexually abused me, but I often wondered what I'd done to make him hurt me. Bewildered and terrified, I'd feel him yank off my tennis shoes, roughly remove my shorts, and force my limbs apart. My ears filled with the sound of him unzipping his pants and the heavy sound of his breathing. When he couldn't sexually abuse me, he spanked and slapped (body), threatened (mind), and demoralized (spirit) me. In my crowded, chaotic child's mind, I had no room for sympathy. At four years old I had no means to leave home. I knew if I were to survive, I'd have to carry my burden alone. My body absorbed this decision, weakening my immune system and making me vulnerable to diabetes, high blood pressure, kidney and thyroid disease, as well as chronic depression, low self-esteem, and recurring thoughts of suicide. I was seventeen years old the last time he beat me with his belt.

His threats cost me the most.

My father threatened that if I told anyone about what "we" were doing, he'd kill my mother. (By using the word "we," my father was able to spread his guilt onto me. Many perpetrators use this kind of language to control their victims.) I took that threat to the depths of my soul. Deeply loving my mother, I wanted to protect her. I felt responsible and an accomplice to a horrific crime.

Researchers Angela Browne and David Finkelhor explain that there is a clinical assumption that children who feel compelled to keep sexual abuse a secret suffer greater psychic distress than victims who disclose the secret and receive assistance and support. I didn't tell anyone about the abuse until I was twenty years old. I was in therapy because I was depressed and suicidal.

My father was a dangerous man, and his legacy made me a dangerous woman.

In reality, I'm very much like him—the anger and rage, the hurt, the loss. At moments, I am overcome by the pain and hurt he suffered as a young boy. I cry for him. He didn't deserve this, and neither did I. Why couldn't he break the cycle of abuse? I was able to; why couldn't he? "Why" questions don't lead to answers—they leave only a profound sense of loss.

The day my father first became sexual with me was the same day I lost my child's sense of innocence. The trauma of my early years seared through my nerves and muscles. The damage was done.

When parents abuse their children, a huge vacuum develops in a child's life, a vacuum that needs to be promptly and permanently filled with help, love, and support. The mending needs to incorporate the mind, body, and spirit. For me, and millions of other children, we didn't have the capacity to know what we needed to heal.

The damage continues to grow as we grow. No wonder our health statistics are so poor.

There are so many little children (in our adult bodies) that cry for love and help.

According to the organization Futures Without Violence, "growing up in a violent home may be a terrifying and traumatic experience that can affect every aspect of a child's life, growth and development." A study of low-income preschoolers found that children who have been exposed to family violence suffer symptoms of post-traumatic stress disorder (PTSD), such as bed-wetting or nightmares, and are at greater risk than their peers of having allergies, asthma, gastrointestinal problems, headaches, and flu. In addition, Browne and Finkelhor found that women who experienced physical abuse as children are at a greater risk of victimization as adults, and men have a far greater (more than double) likelihood of perpetrating abuse.

Several years ago, through the family grapevine, I heard that Mom had asked my father if it were true that he had sexually abused me.

"I don't remember," he answered.

"I don't remember." My father's words haunted me. How could he not remember what he did?

In 1989, I went to work at Hazelden (now known as the Hazelden Betty Ford Foundation), the chemical dependency treatment center in Center City, Minnesota. While I was there, I got a crash course on chemical dependency and the reasons people become dependent on drugs and alcohol. It was possible, a counselor told me, that the alcohol shut down my father's ability to remember and he lost consciousness without losing his ability to move. In chemical dependency terms these are called "blackouts," in which too much alcohol partially or totally robs the drinker's memory.

For me, this seemed even more depressing. He could say, "Oh sorry, kid, I just don't remember doing that while I was drinking." This way, my father could avoid feeling guilty and taking full responsibility for his actions. Though it can help in certain situations, denial often does more harm than good when we refuse to accept the truth. The truth may hurt, but once the family secret is revealed, families can heal and create more authentic behaviors and relationships.

Couldn't he tell he had done something wrong when he came out of the blackout? What about the fact that his pants were below his knees, his penis exposed, and my soiled nightgown on the floor next to his chair? What about the reasons he placed candy under my pillow at night as peace offerings?

Candy. The candy bars Dad gave me were called "Bun" bars. I'd wake up in the morning and find the smashed candy bar under my pillow. The sight caused a mix of guilt and pleasure.

At the age of fifteen, I was diagnosed with insulin-dependent diabetes and was restricted from eating candy. I told myself that I got diabetes because I was a bad girl. I looked at the disease as a form of punishment for being alive and keeping a secret.

Unfortunately, I wound up in the hospital several times because my blood sugar levels were too high. When I was sixteen, I almost succeeded in ending my life. The family doctor was called to our house because I was sick. By the time I was brought to the hospital, my blood sugar level was over 1,600 milligrams. (Normal blood sugar levels are between 80 and 120 milligrams.) I was too sick to know how close I was coming to death.

My father hated hospitals and avoided them whenever possible, so he never visited me. For me, hospitals became a retreat from the abuse. I'd spend days feeling better and better, safe and protected. The abuse would stop for a week or two, but I would return home only to have the abuse cycle begin again.

I started to become depressed, though I didn't know this mental illness by its clinical name for some time. I just thought I was down and that my sense of hopelessness was a periodic occurrence. I gradually became more aware of how often I felt hopeless. I began to brood, and my emotions grew increasingly dark. My feelings of depression were evident in my writing:

> *My eyes open slowly adjusting to the dull throb of morning. I stare at the white, speckled ceiling trying to convince myself to move, but I can't.*
>
> *My body feels like 600 pounds ground into the mattress—too heavy to climb out, too deep to surface.*
>
> *It's another morning, and another bout of depression.*
>
> *I want to cry, but I can't. I'm past the point of tears. I'm terrified and tumbling out-of-control into the nothingness of hopelessness. All I can feel is dread and pain.*
>
> *My bones feel as if they are being twisted and pulled apart. My fingers are swollen like little breakfast sausages. The ache in my lower back is something akin to corporal punishment. The nerves in my head drum to a deafening rock and roll beat.*
>
> *My bed has gone from being my refuge to a torture chamber.*
>
> *I slowly sit up and cringe at the onslaught of memories.*
>
> *I have nothing to get up for.*
>
> *I have nothing to look forward to.*
>
> *I have nothing to get excited about.*
>
> *I have nothing but nothing.*
>
> *I open the blinds and stare out at the day. The sun is shining, the air is fresh with spring, and the neighbors are busy going to work. I shut the blinds and look back at the bed. I want to return to the comfort of the warm sheets but the pain is enough of a deterrent.*
>
> *Why?*
>
> *Why me?*
>
> *Why must I feel this way?*

Why can't I be happy?
Why can't I look forward to a brand new day?
Why must I be depressed?
Again?
Why?

Depression is a pronounced sense of hopelessness causing a tremendous feeling of worthlessness. Depression is a disease and not an issue of willpower. It can be paralyzing and disabling and can turn successful people into failures.

Antidepressants can take away the sharp edges of depression, but they aren't cures for this disease. They aren't "happy pills" that suddenly transform me from a dark brooding creature into a slapstick comedian. It would be a blessing if I could go from sadness to smiles within minutes.

Like many people, when I'm depressed, I sleep. Sleep is an escape from feeling so worthless, but it isn't a cure. In fact, when I awake, I often feel worse, knowing I've lost another day. Failure is written in large, bold letters across the sky.

Depression runs in my family, just like diabetes, cancer, and stroke. Frankly, our gene pool sucks. In addition, of course, alcohol and incest only made matters worse.

I can't remember when the sexual abuse stopped. Most of my memories are jumbled together and difficult to distinguish. There was oral, vaginal, and anal penetration, groping and pain. I didn't want to touch him, and I didn't want him to touch me. I hated the smell of alcohol on his breath, the sound of his ragged breathing, and the feel of his rough hands and whiskers on my naked flesh.

Several times I tried to give myself a black eye so someone would ask me what was going on, but I could never hit myself hard enough to produce a bruise. I even faked a sprained ankle, but still no one asked. I just looked like a normal teenager trying to get attention. I did stupid stuff so that someone could see how troubled I was, but no one ever asked. I loathed myself for the façade I had created.

My father, too, created a façade to hide his rage over his abuse, and it saddens me that I never got to see my father sober and healthy. Instead of mending his mind, body, and spirit, he chose alcohol to lessen his pain and hide from his nightmares.

I hid too. I went deep inside myself and hid behind my bones, organs, muscles, nerves, and skin. The storm of emotions I felt gave me migraines, elevated my blood sugars and blood pressure, and sent my endocrine system into a whirlwind. I didn't talk about the abuse, so my body took the hit of the trauma. My mind closed the door and locked it. My spirit was gone.

All the while the abuse was happening, my mind and body were reacting and trying to attain a state of homeostasis, but I had little fuel to keep running.

I wanted to give up. I wanted to die.

Instead, I began looking at the things that helped me survive during all those years, and I discovered I had some tools to work with. I didn't call them "tools" right away. This came later in my healing. Nevertheless, they are the hammers, levels, scissors, and saws I used, and still use today, to move beyond trauma and illness as I built my life.

Tools to Cope with Childhood Sexual Abuse

The following tools incorporate the mind-body-spirit connection. They may not be the tools you prefer to use to help yourself, but they will give you some inspiration to design your own tool kit.

1. Embrace honesty. It took years before I could face what my father had done and the threats he made to me. It was difficult to

tell someone because I didn't trust anyone inside or outside my family. But I knew I couldn't start to heal if I wasn't honest with myself. Where do you start being honest with yourself and others? Many of us lie for different reasons. Sometimes it's a little white lie to keep from hurting someone else's feelings. Most of us lie to avoid arguments or pain. Whatever the reason, you need to stop lying because it causes people to distrust you and can become a habitual problem with serious consequences. Start by being honest with yourself.

2. Write your own fear story. Louise L. Hay's book *Heal Your Body: The Mental Causes for Physical Illness and the Metaphysical Way to Overcome Them* was a lifesaver for me. I learned that if I wanted to eliminate a condition for good, I had to resolve past causes such as trauma, loss, and illness. For me that meant going into my past to find out what happened and what went wrong. I was angry and criticized myself every time something wasn't good enough. I discovered I was making myself sick.

Soon after I learned I had sleep apnea, caused by a narrowed throat (for more on sleep apnea, see Chapter 11), I knew in a moment of clarity it was due, in part, to my unwillingness to tell my story about the sexual, emotional, and physical abuse I had endured. My throat was literally closing because of my silence. I couldn't remain silent any longer. I vowed I would start sharing my life story with others. I had to tell others what I'd been through, and I needed to heal myself by opening my heart and letting the resentment and anger go.

"I'm ugly. I'm stupid. I'm unlovable." Where the heck did these messages come from? One night, as I worked on an assignment for my Renewing Life facilitator certification, I was asked to write my own fear story. I never dreamed this writing exercise would be so powerful.

My Fear Story

My father began sexually, physically, and emotionally abusing me when I was four years old. During the abuse, he would say things to me such as "you're dirty" or "you're dumb." He said I would always be a failure and unlovable.

I grew up fearing I would be just like he said. I went overboard trying to always be clean and fresh smelling. I felt I couldn't go anywhere without wearing a clean-smelling perfume.

My life has been spotted with unsuccessful relationships. I always felt I wasn't good enough, that my partners were so much better than me. I wasn't pretty enough and I wasn't smart enough. Even though partners loved me, I didn't feel like they loved me enough. I felt like a fake and a failure.

Through years of therapy and introspection, I came to the realization that all my fears were those of my father's. They were never mine! It amazes me how deeply I absorbed his fears. His fears were constantly draining me.

When I was diagnosed with cancer, I knew his fears (now mine) were weakening my immune system. I had to stop the fears before they killed me.

Write your own fear story with honesty. You'll be amazed at what you learn about yourself and how you can heal your trauma.

3. Get therapy. I was nineteen years old when I first went into therapy. The results were not at all what I had expected. The college counselor I saw sexually exploited me in my senior year of college. The "real" therapy started when I was twenty-three. By then my life was a disaster. I couldn't keep relationships. I lied and hurt others with my anger, and I hated my life. From what seemed like the very bottom of life, I went to see another therapist—terrified that my prior experience with therapy would be repeated. Yet, from

that second appointment, I learned to trust myself and tell my story. I told my story and talked about my fears. I wept for hours at a time and got angry. Luckily, this time I had someone who understood the anger and helped me through it. I've had many therapists over the years because of insurance changes, but I've always gone back in and told my story. The repetition helped because the more I talked, the more relief I felt. I walked carefully into my memories and waded through the muck. There were times when I thought the muck would consume me, but my therapist was always there to help me out. Dealing with sexual abuse is dirty business. To survive I had to roll up my sleeves and get working. I highly recommend using therapy as a tool. Ask your friends if they know of a reputable therapist. Yes, there are bad ones out there, so be careful. If you meet with a therapist and you don't feel right about him or her, your body is telling you to stop. Check out another therapist and as many therapists as you need to. Telling your story to a trusted person will help you heal. Many therapists work on a sliding-fee scale, and some clinics offer low-cost or even free therapy. If you're employed, find out if you are covered under your employer's mental health plan.

4. Write. James W. Pennebaker, of the University of Texas at Austin, is a pioneer in linking the effects of writing about traumatic events to improved immune system function. Like many great innovations, it was born out of personal experience. He began writing about his depression and then noticed the beneficial effects. Pennebaker's work is mentioned in Kieron Devlin's essay "Writing as Healing: A Pen Is Mightier Than a Pill." Writing can be healing, so try writing in a journal each day. You'll start to see patterns, and you'll be able to change behaviors you dislike in yourself.

5. Reveal family secrets. Child abuse has been around for centuries, yet many families are adamant about keeping the abuse from the public at all costs. Does the public really need to know? Yes! How can we stop child abuse if we remain silent? The voices of

abused children need to be heard—loudly. Being silent only adds more trauma and loss to its victims.

Children living in an abusive family share the same guilt and shame whether they were abused or not. Feeling protective of their family, many siblings of children who were abused hold onto denial. But keeping the family secret creates mental illness issues like depression (which in this case is unexpressed anger) and anxiety.

Sadly, those of us who reveal family secrets are often further victimized. Our truth telling is frequently met with anger and rage. I spent years agonizing over the decision to talk publicly about the abuse; I knew there would be consequences. I revealed our family's physical, sexual, and emotional abuse to get help and to help others, but instead I became the target of much anger and blame. But if I had to do it over again, I would still make the same choice. I believe my honesty has saved my life.

We don't have to get sick because we fear the consequences of speaking up. In order to bring healing into our lives, we must move away from secrets that make us ill, and we must learn how to cope with our suffering. Keeping secrets damages our minds, bodies, and spirits. Denial increases the trauma and loss. Many studies conclude that revealing such pain helps us heal from abuse.

To confront denial takes courage. To forgive is heroic. To live openly is priceless.

6. Laugh. When I can laugh, I know I can survive any situation. I'm lucky because my whole family has a great sense of humor. We always laugh. Humor saved us. There's absolutely nothing funny about incest and abuse, but watching a funny movie, going to a comedy club, or being around friends who can laugh are great sources of healing.

Restful sleep, exercise, and proper nutrition are key ingredients of a healthy lifestyle, but what about the cackle, chuckle, and guffaw? According to wellness experts Leslie Ahern and Paul Antokolsky, "laughing is as essential to good health as any diet plan, workout routine, or prescription remedy." Antokolsky refers to a study showing that laughing for only ten minutes a day reduced blood pressure and pain from arthritis.

Laughter brings oxygen into all the cells in our bodies, which we need for energy and vitality, lowering our blood pressure, reducing pain levels, and helping our cholesterol at the same time. Not only that, but it's just fun to do. I love to laugh.

7. Work on your resilience. Studies have shown that sexually abused children are more likely to develop a range of emotional and health problems, including depression, PTSD, and suicidal thoughts. As adults, we're more likely to be unemployed, homeless, addicted to drugs or alcohol, and alone. So what about the adults who survived child sexual abuse and are employed, have a home, aren't addicted to drugs and alcohol, and have many friends? Like me, they used their ability to bounce back (resilience) over and over again.

Resilience is an internal springboard that helps us bounce back from threatening circumstances. An object falls from a window several floors above you. As it hits the sidewalk, you jump back away from it. That's physical resilience. A stranger tries to steal your purse, but you run for help. That's physical resilience.

Someone tells you about the sudden death of a loved one. You instantly cry, letting your feelings out. That's emotional resilience. A friend tells you how wonderful you are. Your heart feels as if it's going to explode. That's emotional resilience. If we are resilient, we are comfortable with our feelings and express emotions in healthy ways, and we know how to control our fear, anxiety, or sadness.

Today's research proves that resilient people are optimistic, happy, healthy, productive, have better communication with others, succeed more, and are less likely to become depressed than people who are pessimistic. Resilience is about seeing yourself and situations as optimistically as you can—but within the bounds of reality.

A key factor in resilience is having self-confidence. If you're confident and can cope with what life throws in your path, your self-esteem will follow. Resilient people are connected with others, have close friends, and can show empathy. Empathy serves resilience by facilitating strong relationships (a support system) that they can turn to when they need help.

Examples of resilience include the ability to change your attitude about feeling like "damaged goods" to an image more positive like being a "thriver." I keep a list of all of my accomplishments, so when I feel down I can remind myself that I'm a "winner." Asking questions is also another expression of resilience. I'm learning to ask good who, what, where, when, and how questions so I can get specific answers.

8. Express your anger. Anger is a tool you can use in your healing process, but you've got to be willing to express it. I found expressing anger to be one of the most difficult things to do. Sure, I tried slugging a pillow in therapy, but it always felt as if my anger was bouncing off the material and hitting me in the face. It took me fifty years to finally scream out, "Fuck you! Fuck you, Dad, for messing up my life!" I know the word "fuck" is offensive to some people, but saying it was a powerful thing for me to do. If another word works better for you, then use it. When you release the stress and tension that are hiding behind your organs and muscles, you're telling your body and mind to relax and to stay balanced. I strongly suggest working with a professional to help you express your anger appropriately. Don't mess around with anger because it can come back to bite you. There are appropriate techniques you can use to express your rage and anger, and a professional can help you practice those techniques before you hurt yourself or others.

ACTIVITY 4

Release Emotions Through Writing

SUPPLIES: pencil or pen and paper, or a computer

Consider a traumatic event or chronic stress you may have experienced in childhood—or any topic that makes you angry. If you can't remember a trauma or highly stressful event from childhood, take an event from your adulthood. Set a timer for one minute, and write or type continuously about what you remember.

Do not pause to think. Do not worry about spelling, grammar, punctuation, or anything else. Just write! It can be a mumble-jumble of thoughts and emotions. Get your feelings out. Describe your feelings. Describe your environment. Recall any words people may have said to you. Write whatever comes into your head. No pauses. On your mark, get set, go!

Reflect on these questions by yourself or with friends:

- Was this difficult to do?
- Were you able to release some painful feelings?
- What were some of the emotions you felt?
- What tools do you have to heal yourself as an adult?

THEN   NOW

Healing from Rape

I didn't date a lot in high school. Having a boyfriend wasn't important to me—playing on the girls' golf and basketball teams was my passion. I was also very active in student government. I had a close female friend or two, but it was very hard for me to have a personal relationship with someone. In high school I was more like everyone's friend.

In college, the trend among the women students was to have a boyfriend to go to football games and parties. My perception was that you weren't "cool" if you didn't have a date on Friday and Saturday nights. I so wanted to be cool and liked by other people. One weekend my freshman year, I went to a bar with some friends and met a sophomore.

I thought he was a cool person, so I went out with him for three weeks. I did notice how demanding he got when he drank too much beer, but from my father's example, I just figured that this was something guys did. One night, he invited me over to his dorm room to watch TV. I thought his roommate would be there. The minute I entered his room, I knew I shouldn't have come. He was already drunk. He ripped off my shirt and forced me onto his bed. When he forced my legs apart, a little voice inside of me screamed: NOT AGAIN!

I was raped.

I fell into a deep, dark hole.

For days I could hardly move or think. I was terrified to go into the dining hall for fear I'd see him. I told no one what had happened because I was too ashamed and afraid that people would say I asked for it, that it was my fault, that I was dirty. Then the harassing phone calls started. For a week, the phone would ring at three a.m. It would be some of his friends jeering me and calling me a whore. It didn't take long for me to not answer the phone, and it was clear he took no responsibility for his actions that night.

I began to unravel.

I cried. I had nightmares and flashbacks. I got migraines and wouldn't leave my dorm room at night. My body and mind were telling me to get help, but I was so scared. I felt I couldn't stop the abuse. I saw myself as a victim who would continue to be victimized.

I also suffered a ruptured disc in my back during this time. I was playing touch football, and someone from the opposing team landed on top of me. The pain was excruciating. I went to the emergency room at the hospital and got painkillers. The medication was so powerful it made two weeks fly by without notice, and it made the pain from the rape tolerable. The rape went into my body and hid behind my organs, muscles, and nerves. Instead of dealing with the rape in a healthy way, I got pain medication. The doctors in the emergency room didn't know I had been raped, so they refilled my prescription for medication without question. Sure, I had a real problem. I had a ruptured disc—the x-rays proved that, and I had a good explanation for the damage. But I was ripe for accidents: my body, mind, and spirit were overwhelmed by trauma.

Pain is a warning sign. If you heed the warning and take proper action, the discomfort usually stops, and the problem can be corrected. If you ignore the warning, you can suffer permanent damage.

I didn't go into therapy right after the rape. With no immediate support or help, I let the rape seep into my body, where it took root and began to cause problems. Emotionally I was a wreck. Hopelessness became my constant companion. I was put on academic probation that first semester and continued to do poorly in my studies for another year. During my sophomore year, I began to study in earnest because the result of being kicked out of college and becoming homeless was enough motivation to keep me going.

My mind kept replaying the rape repeatedly, and when I got more comfortable with the trauma, my mind threw in memories of my father just to make things more interesting. I felt like trash. My self-esteem and self-confidence took permanent residence in the toilet. I was angry, depressed, and hopeless.

Luckily, there was a woman in my dormitory who was supportive of my struggles. I finally told her about the rape. That led to telling her about my father. Little by little I started trusting her, and we became close friends. We were both surprised when our feelings deepened and we fell in love, but we kept this love a secret because we were concerned about people's reactions.

Cathy was a lifesaver for me. A brilliant and creative woman, she listened to my stories for hours and never made a judgment. I opened my heart and my soul to her, and she made me feel that I mattered. I finally found someone who loved me—baggage and all.

She encouraged me to follow my heart. I was taking creative writing classes and, at first, felt totally unworthy. She read my pieces and gave me positive feedback. She helped me to stretch my mind and widen my studies to expand my views. Cathy also taught me how to study. Ultimately she helped me make the dean's list.

Cathy was an angel of mercy. She helped me to finally see that life wasn't always so harsh. Bad things happened, but her love and support helped me survive. I am forever grateful to her.

Tools to Cope with Rape

Though recent surveys have found a decline in rape cases, the numbers are still horrific. According to the Rape, Abuse and Incest National Network (RAINN), 17.7 million American women have been victims of rape or attempted rape. About 44 percent of rape victims are under age eighteen, and 80 percent are under the age of thirty. Group statistics take away from the pain incurred by individuals. It's not easy getting over a rape. Many people find surviving a rape to be a daily challenge. From flashbacks and night terrors to feelings of vulnerability, we try to put our lives back together and move forward. After a rape many victims know life will never be kind, and the feeling of being secure and safe is unreachable.

The following tools helped me cope with the trauma from rape.

1. Prayer. I'm a spiritual woman. I don't believe you have to go to a church, synagogue, mosque, or temple to pray for help and guidance. If you find it helpful, you can say your prayers in the presence of a priest, minister, or rabbi. No matter the object of your prayer (be it God, Allah, Buddha, the Great Spirit, the Universe, or Higher Power), you can unload your sorrows and pain onto a force greater than yourself. I often imagine that I'm being held in the palms of the Great Spirit. Here I am protected and nourished. I can scream about my pain and cry until there are no more tears. I can heal in this safe place. My prayers have no structure because I believe rambling is cathartic and the Great Spirit knows what I'm saying anyway. The prayers come from my soul, and I can voice my fears knowing that the Universe is listening.

Did I sometimes blame the Great Spirit for the rape? Sure, it's a natural response to trauma. Once I moved past blaming, I started healing. I find that I pray best when I'm alone and feeling safe. I've developed a very close relationship with the Great Spirit over the years. Upon waking in the morning, I give thanks to the Great Spirit for another day of life.

2. Self-defense classes. Take a self-defense class, and find out the best ways to stay safe. You may think self-defense is a karate kick to the groin or jab in the eyes of an attacker, but in reality self-defense means doing everything possible to *avoid* fighting someone who threatens or attacks you. Self-defense is about using your head—not your fists. If you feel threatened and fight back, you may actually risk making a situation worse. People who attack may be high on drugs or alcohol with their adrenaline pumping like crazy. Fighting back may make them even more angry and violent. The best way to handle any attack or threat of attack is to yell and try to get away. You're less likely to be injured. Self-defense classes focus on how to prevent an assault. They teach you how to avoid a potential attack before it happens by trusting your instincts. Your intuition and common sense can help get you out of trouble. You can develop a strong mindset so that you can literally voice your rage and attract attention. I've been to several classes in the years since I was raped. I've learned to voice my rage in threatening situations.

3. Life-affirming messages. Negative messages are based in fear, which is debilitating. Take a closer look at your fears. Are they yours? Did they come from someone else? What is each fear really saying to you? Fear is a secondary feeling, much like an iceberg. What's beneath the surface? Is it a feeling of hurt or rejection? Anger? Start to eliminate the fear by creating life-affirming messages like "I am free to express my feelings. I express my anger in appropriate ways. I am loved." Replace life-draining messages with confidence-boosting ones. When I'm feeling depressed, I talk to myself and remind myself that I'm a survivor. I'm strong and will not let depression ruin my day. I acknowledge that the depression is there, but I won't feed it the way I used to. I reframe things that make me feel more alive. Focusing on life-affirming messages is crucial when dealing with abuse

issues. "Change your mind; change your life." There's a lot of truth to that saying.

Remember you can't feel fear and love at the same time. Live in the present, and choose love over fear.

4. Music. I love to listen to music. There are certain notes that open my heart and soul to let in the healing. I listen to a lot of instrumental music so that words don't interrupt my thinking. I've also found that certain notes open certain chakras (energy points).

Chakras, mentioned in ancient Hindu texts of knowledge, are known as energy points or spots located in the human body. There are seven chakras, vertically aligned in the center of the body; they start at the base of the spine and go up to the crown of the head. They are commonly known as the root, sacral, solar plexus, heart, throat, third eye, and crown chakras, although they also have other names.

According to one theory of chakras, the body's health is dependent on balancing these energy points for good circulation and blood flow. In closed positions, the chakras block needed energy from flowing through the body. In the open position, chakras allow energy to move freely back and forth. Symptoms of blocked chakras are a lack of energy and stamina, anxiety, and not feeling able to cope.

Chakras are reported to be sensitive to sound. The root chakra is linked with the musical note C, the sacral chakra with D, the solar plexus with E, the heart chakra with F, the throat chakra with G, the third eye chakra with A, and the crown chakra with B.

When my chakras open, I tend to cry suddenly. But it's a wonderful feeling that I know lowers my blood pressure. The notes flow around my organs, muscles, and nerves, giving me a feeling of buoyancy, freedom, and healing. If you really enjoy music, chakra healing may be for you.

5. Reading. Several weeks after I was raped, my mind thirsted for knowledge. I went to the university's library to find books on

rape. I wanted to know the statistics—I wanted to know I wasn't alone. I wanted to learn how women survived rape and went on with their lives. I wanted to know the aftereffects of rape and ways to handle them. Along with therapy, books gave me the background information about rape that I needed to heal. I read stories written by survivors. Their stories helped me get through the numbness I felt. As I read, I got angry and cried for these women as much as I cried for myself. I also recommend listening to audiobooks. You may find a voice reading aloud to be comforting.

6. Relocate. I moved away from the city where I was raped and sexually exploited. Assault and violence can be found anywhere and everywhere, but I needed to get out of the city where the trauma occurred. I needed to start over. Though relocating is physically and spiritually draining, the benefits are extremely healing. You're not running away or giving up. You've made the decision to take care of yourself. Start by researching places you'd like to move to, and then review your finances to see what you can afford. Making the choice to move and deciding for yourself where to live can be empowering and healing.

If you're a victim of rape, know that with the right type of support, encouragement, and love, you can heal!

ACTIVITY 5

Reflect on *The Scream*
by Edvard Munch

SUPPLIES: pens or colored pencils

The Norwegian artist Edvard Munch painted *The Scream* in 1893; it was his most famous work. Here I've reproduced the central image of the painting: a figure screaming with their hands to their head. Take some time to consider the figure, and then respond to the questions below.

We tend to be afraid of painful feelings and memories. Releasing them is important. Choose some colors to represent your feelings and memories, and color around the figure. Think of the colors as releasing the painful memories from your body, mind, and spirit.

➤ If you were the figure in the painting, what are you feeling?

➤ Does this stimulate a particular memory?

➤ What are you screaming about?

The Nightmare of Sexual Exploitation

As a little girl I had a very real monster in my life. I escaped him and went to college. When I was eighteen, another very real monster emerged.

This monster was thirty-one years older than I, nice looking with sparkling gray eyes, and a therapist. I went into therapy scared but with the hope that I could become whole again. My life was so fragmented that I couldn't find any patterns or resources to help me through the pain. I wanted to feel better. I longed for friends I could trust and a healthy relationship with someone. I wanted the night terrors to end. Most of all, I wanted never to be abused again.

My first appointment turned into four years of therapy. Yet, when I graduated from the university, my life was completely out of control. Suicide was the only way I could see to end the pain in my life.

The university's therapist who sexually exploited me was a prominent figure in the community; she had a doctorate in psychology and was the center's associate director. After several sessions, I began to feel a certain trust.

Growing up I believed all monsters were male. I believed that women could never hurt me the way men could. This mistaken belief only contributed to my fears and feelings of isolation, agony, and shame. I feared, just as with the rape, that people would say I led her on and that I was responsible. I feared that people would dismiss my pain because women didn't sexually exploit other women, or it would be written off as just a "gay issue."

Eventually I learned that sexual exploitation, like abuse and rape, is an issue of power—the need to control. It is extremely traumatic to the victim and comes with its own set of unhealthy effects, including illness.

My therapist knew what my issues were and where I was most vulnerable. She knew I had problems establishing healthy boundaries and that I had difficulty saying no. She knew about all my ghosts, and she turned around and abused me, too.

According to an article by Linda Mabus Jorgenson, up to 12 percent of therapists admit in confidential self-reports to sexual involvement with at least one patient. Some researchers believe that the actual incidence is higher.

The first time my therapist was intimate with me I was shocked. Frankly, I never expected to be hit on by a therapist—male or female. Though I had no other therapy experience to compare it to, I knew it was wrong. She invited me to her house, where we would drink wine and listen to music, all the while we talked about our needs and wants. We had dinners and long conversations that made me feel special. She said she was still recovering from the abrupt end of a relationship with a graduate student at the university, who was now dating my English professor. The therapist was hurt, and I tried my best to make her laugh and forget her pain. We'd talk for hours on the phone when we couldn't get together. My therapy now became hugging and kissing sessions.

At one point, the therapist asked me to promise that I wouldn't tell anyone about what was going on between us. She told me that if someone found out and reported her, it would be "professional suicide" for her. She would lose her job at the center, and she had no other way to support herself financially. I kept quiet. I didn't even tell Cathy, who by this time was my partner, what was happening, but Cathy saw past the lies I created. She told me that having sex with my therapist was wrong. My relationship with Cathy started to disintegrate, and I asked her if we could "just be friends." She knew what the therapist was doing to me and was angry about my affair. I hurt Cathy terribly, and the shame I felt was immense, but I continued to see the therapist.

During the four months the therapist was sexual with me, I was elated and depressed; I was emotionally high and physically drained. I loved her and hated myself. I wanted it to continue, and I prayed for it to end.

When my therapy came to an abrupt end, I was devastated. I had gone home for my sister's wedding, and when I returned, I tried to contact the therapist, but she refused to answer my calls. I tried to see her at the center, but I was told she had no appointments available. I was blacklisted from the only place and the only person who I believed could help me.

I fell into a huge black hole. I had no dreams. I felt used and had nowhere to turn. I couldn't turn to Cathy for comfort because I had caused her so much pain. It became another dark time in my life. I knew in my heart that I had hurt Cathy deeply.

I finally moved back home and spent my days and nights looking for answers. When I told my mother what happened, she encouraged me to see a psychiatrist, but the suggestion only frightened me more and deepened my despair. There were no guarantees that this episode wouldn't happen again.

After two months of staying with my parents, I found a job in Minneapolis and moved. I wanted so desperately to start a new life. I tried to establish another relationship, but I hurt my new partner, too.

I believed that if someone had sex with me, then that meant they loved me. So the more people I had sex with, the more love I felt. This faulty thinking left a trail of shattered relationships and broken hearts. I always felt like a loser. My guilt and shame was over my head, and I was drowning. I couldn't forgive myself for hurting two very wonderful women.

I couldn't trust anyone—not even myself. I had become a monster.

The stress and strain caused my blood sugar to climb, and toward the end of my senior year in college I was hospitalized because this stressful situation elevated my blood sugar and made me sick.

It took me two years before I found the courage to go back into therapy. I was fortunate to find a very wonderful therapist. At our first session, I was shocked when she said to me, "Alex, I'm not going to be sexual with you." I felt relieved at her statement but shameful that I couldn't save myself from being a victim. So many negative emotions flashed through my mind and body. It was now time for me to work on the repercussions of having been sexually exploited.

After thirteen years of therapy, I was able to build my self-confidence and self-esteem. I began trusting a few more people, and I am now in a very stable marriage. I'd like to say that trust issues and low self-esteem don't affect me anymore, but they do. Luckily, I now have the tools to help me get beyond the "bad girl" image.

I found enough courage to file a formal complaint with the Department of Regulation and Licensing in the state where the sexual exploitation occurred. Though I was told that my complaint warranted an investigation, the Licensing Board could not take action against the therapist because she did not hold a license by the Psychology Board in that state.

To add insult to injury, several weeks after receiving the board's letter with their decision, I read an article about my therapist. Her photo caught my attention. The article stated she was doing volunteer work with sex offenders. My adverse reaction to the article took many therapy sessions to overcome. I was fortunate, however, to have a solid support system in place so that I didn't get lost in that black hole again.

The silence surrounding sexual exploitation by therapists, clergy, and health care professionals has been going on for centuries. The cases that have come to light regarding the Catholic Church have brought sexual exploitation and sexual abuse issues to the forefront. I'm ecstatic that the voices of those who have been hurt are now being heard. It's time to create a community where acts of sexual exploitation and misconduct are not tolerated. No matter what kind of abuse—sexual abuse, incest, rape, sexual exploitation—the results are the same. Lives are forever changed.

If you are the victim of sexual exploitation, do not be ashamed. Remember that it is an issue of power—someone you trusted took advantage of your situation and turned it into sexual trauma. It doesn't matter how the therapist, medical provider, or other person in authority made it seem okay. It's not. Sexual exploitation is wrong, and you have the right to report the perpetrator. Trauma like this often gets ugly, but remember that your reputation is just as important as theirs. Keeping the abuse secret is only going to hurt you. When you hear the words "Don't tell anyone," that's a good indication that whatever the behavior is, it's wrong.

I believe we must publicly expose sexual exploitation. Victims are not responsible for ruining these professionals!

Tools to Cope with Sexual Exploitation

The tools I used to help me through sexual exploitation are the same ones I used for childhood abuse and rape. Tools like honesty, therapy, and resilience work very well in these instances. I also used these tools:

1. Reporting my story. When a situation doesn't seem right, trust your instincts. Our minds and bodies alert us to potential danger. You can also talk to someone familiar with the situation but outside it and ask for guidance. Report authority figures that hurt or threaten you. If it's a therapist, psychologist, psychiatrist, or member of the clergy, report it to the police. Sexual abuse is not your fault.

2. Exercise. I like to take a walk with a friend or get on the treadmill to cope with stress from trauma. The physical effort calms me. I try to walk every day whether I feel like it or not. My dog, Bob, helps to keep me walking because he needs to walk, too.

According to the article "Can Exercise Make Me High?" physical activity has a documented effect on our emotional reactions to stress. Fit people are usually in high spirits after a lengthy exercise, sometimes to the point of elation or joy. This feeling is associated with the presence of endorphins, which are released by the pituitary gland in the brain: "Endorphins are the body's natural pain reliever. It may be that the brain interprets exercise as a form of 'pain' or it may be that the increase in fatty acids caused by long, gentle exercise acidifies the blood, which triggers the release of endorphins. In any case, you can get from exercise a natural high, similar to a drug high but with none of the bad side effects."

3. Meditation. One of my wonderful therapists suggested that I listen to meditation tapes to help me with my lack of self-confidence and self-esteem. I've taken classes, and I listen to recordings. I find meditation to be a source of relaxation and calm. My mind becomes

clearer, and I can recall names, places, and memories. I've listened to meditation tapes to cope with stress and to fight cancer.

The most productive source of research on meditation since 1970 has been the Transcendental Meditation movement (TM). Many of the effects visible to researchers of TM are enjoyed by practitioners of any of the many nonstriving, restful, open methods of meditation. According to the book *Meditation as Medicine*:

- Meditation creates a unique hypometabolic state, in which the metabolism is in an even deeper state of rest than during sleep. During sleep, oxygen consumption drops by 8 percent, but during meditation, it drops by 10 to 20 percent.
- Meditation is the only activity that reduces blood lactate, a marker of stress and anxiety.
- The calming hormones melatonin and serotonin are increased by meditation, and the stress hormone cortisol is decreased.
- Meditation has a profound effect upon three key indicators of aging: hearing ability, blood pressure, and vision of close objects.
- Long-term meditators experience 80 percent less heart disease and 50 percent less cancer than nonmeditators.

You can find a variety of meditation recordings online or at your local bookstore. I highly recommend the recordings produced by Belleruth Naparstek, a psychotherapist, author, and guided imagery innovator.

4. Antidepressants. I am not a pill pusher. My intention here is to shed some light on how antidepressants have helped me survive trauma. Not everyone needs antidepressants, but if you find that

hopelessness and despair are your only companions, see a doctor, or talk with your therapist about medication options.

Antidepressants can improve your mood, sleep, appetite, and concentration. You may need to try more than one kind before finding what works best for you. My experience with antidepressants is that they help take the sharp edge off my depression so I can function more clearly. I still can feel depressed, but I'm not in that horrible black hole that makes everything seem impossible.

I fought going on antidepressants for years. I thought I could manage my depression without medication. I was also embarrassed that my therapist recommended it. In fact, two different therapists suggested I go on antidepressants. Over time, my depression wore me down, and during a week of immense despair, I finally agreed to try an antidepressant. I've now been on an antidepressant for over two decades. I don't feel addicted; it's more like taking insulin for my diabetes. It's just something that makes me feel more stable and healthy. The bottom line is that antidepressants are a good tool for those intrusive suicidal thoughts. I don't want to end up a statistic. I want to live. When my doctor feels I'm ready, I'll give up this antidepressant.

5. Deep breathing. Sometimes when I deal with a crisis or trauma, my breathing becomes shallow, which deprives my body of oxygen. I learned that it's natural to feel that I'm not myself after a major—or even minor—trauma. With deep breathing, I can accept my reactions so that I can feel better and process things more easily. Breathing deeply is one of the most difficult tools I've learned to use. When trauma strikes, I don't have the patience to heal. I want to go back to the way I was. I'm always ready to return to "normal." Trauma, however, takes time to process through the mind, body, and spirit. My spirit may recover more quickly than my mind and body, but I have to wait for all three to heal before I retain my

sense of balance. I can't hurry the mind, body, or spirit to get over a trauma. So I work on deep breathing. Taking several deep breaths is a wonderful way to calm anxiety and slow me down when I'm in a panic. I try to slow my heartbeat and concentrate on the air filling my lungs. I don't always remember to breathe, so it's helpful when friends remind me.

ACTIVITY 6

Draw the Connection Between Stress/Trauma and Illness

SUPPLIES: pen or pencil and paper, or a computer

Chronic stress and trauma leave an imprint on our psychophysiology and contribute to illness. Events may have occurred years before the illness appears. This activity is to help you consider possible connections between chronic stress, trauma, and illness in your life.

List up to three illnesses or diseases you have experienced in your life, along with the approximate date it occurred or was diagnosed. Then list any prolonged or chronic stress or trauma that happened before the illness occurred. Add any additional brief comments or observations you have.

For example:

YEAR	ILLNESS	PREVIOUS STRESS/TRAUMA
1961	Kidney Infection	Sexual Abuse
1972	Diabetes	Physical & Emotional Abuse
1989	Graves' Disease (Thyroid)	Relationship Break-up

YEAR	ILLNESS	PREVIOUS STRESS/TRAUMA

Now select one of your illnesses, and write briefly about how you coped with it. Did you see a doctor? If so, what questions did they ask? How did you handle any stress related to the illness?

NEVER GIVE UP

3

Strengthening Your Immune System after Injury and Illness

Osteoarthritis Defense

Osteoarthritis, also called degenerative joint disease, is the most common type of arthritis. It's associated with a breakdown of cartilage in joints and can occur in almost any joint in the body. It most commonly occurs in the weight-bearing joints of the hips, knees, and spine. It can also affect the fingers, thumb, neck, and large toe. It usually does not affect other joints unless previous injury or excessive stress is involved. According to "The Basic Facts of Osteoarthritis" on WebMD.com:

> Osteoarthritis causes the cartilage in a joint to become stiff and lose its elasticity, making it more susceptible to damage. Over time, the cartilage may wear away in some areas, greatly decreasing its ability to act as a shock absorber. As the cartilage deteriorates, tendons and ligaments stretch, causing pain. If the condition worsens, the bones could rub against each other.

As a kid I was the neighborhood tomboy. I loved being active and was always on the street playing kickball, in the field throwing a football, or in the driveway shooting a basketball. If I was outside,

I was happy and away from trouble at home. Sports gave me a good excuse to be outside, and I looked for opportunities to be active. As I grew, my interests turned more toward golf and softball. I played on a softball team through my twenties and thirties. During my last game of softball, I dislocated my right shoulder on a stupid dive for a ball hit down the third baseline. I had previously dislocated my left shoulder, too. It was time for me to hang up my glove and cleats.

In my mid-forties I was diagnosed with osteoarthritis—a painful condition in my fingers, shoulders, hips, and feet. Heredity, injury, and joint overuse are all causes of osteoarthritis. But if I consider what my body remembers, I wonder if my joints did indeed take the impact of my abuses.

"Oh, come on, Alex, are you going to blame all your medical conditions on the abuse you suffered?" I ask myself. There are those who feel that I'm making a stretch here. But it's a fact that trauma weakens the immune system, making the body more vulnerable to illness and disease. Scientific data associates traumatic stress with adverse health effects. Studies prove physiological alterations from PTSD (post-traumatic stress disorder) correlate with predictable diseases seen in people with the diagnosis.

Osteoarthritis is one of the most common among the over hundred types of arthritis, but the diagnosis can still be a shock. No one wants to find out that there's something wrong with their body. In my case, I sat in my doctor's office in stunned silence. It was another diagnosis added to my growing list of medical problems.

Too much is still too much. In order to complete the grieving process I had to deal with anger, hurt, and pain. Men may typically express anger but not hurt, while women typically express hurt but not anger. It's easier for me to admit that I am hurt than I am angry. Studies show that we learn our responses to anger between the ages of three and five years old. Between ages three and five, I watched what my father did when he was angry. He yelled. He threw things.

He broke things. He hit me. When my mother was angry, she emotionally withdrew or chose the silent treatment.

I adopted my mother's silent treatment as a mechanism to express my anger. I thought for a long time that it was a less abusive choice, but looking back, I can see how wrong this assumption was. The silent treatment is abusive. When you're on the receiving end, it feels like total, absolute rejection. It leaves no physical scars, but it does leave emotional ones.

I know now that I needed to say I was angry about having osteoarthritis. I also know that I needed to understand that anger is normal. What can make anger destructive is how it is expressed. Clearly, my parents did not have healthy ways of expressing their anger. People can learn to express anger in healthy ways through anger management classes. Coping with anger about osteoarthritis may seem unimportant, but it's actually a huge part of coping with the condition itself.

Tools for Coping with Osteoarthritis

Below are some tools I've found helpful as I've learned to live with osteoarthritis.

1. Talking and listening. I know this may sound silly, but I talk to my joints when they're hurting. I visualize I'm having a conversation with them. I say, "Okay, joints, you're really hurting today. What's up with that? Is it the weather? Did I strain you in some way? How can I help you feel better?" Then I listen carefully for what my joints need. Believe it or not, they tell me. They tell me I need to take a hot bath or take some Advil. They tell me to put my feet up or get a heating pad or a cold pack. When I'm really in pain, my joints will even tell me when I need to see my doctor. It really is amazing how our bodies will tell us what they need. We just have to listen carefully.

2. Exercising. I've mentioned this tool before, but I'm bringing it up again. Exercise supports the mind-body-spirit connection. When my body hurts, my mind is screaming for a painkiller, and my spirit is flat, I get off my butt and go for a walk or get on the treadmill. I start out slowly, allowing my muscles and joints to warm up. I try to concentrate on taking in deep breaths to deal with the pain. When I can get my mind and body in sync, I then work on my spirit. I tell myself I'm strong. I tell myself that my joints and muscles are water-filled, and I can move in a graceful, fluid motion. Once I warm up, I stretch my hands, arms, legs, knees, neck and shoulders, feet and ankles, and spinal cord.

3. Practicing qigong. Pronounced "chee gung," qigong is an ancient Chinese healing art that helps increase the flow of energy throughout your body. Through slow movements and conscious breathing, qigong can help you relax and balance your energy. It's also been found to strengthen the immune system. According to the Tiantian School of qigong:

> Qigong offers an effective way to supplement health care regimens and return to an optimal state of well-being. Regular qigong practice has been scientifically proven in studies all over the world to cure and prevent illness. Once health is regained, qigong becomes an anti-aging technique and a discipline to balance the emotions and explore the potentials of the mind. How does this happen? It happens for one very simple reason: the condition of the physical body is a direct result of the condition of the energetic body. Change the quality of the energy in and around the body and the physical body works to "match" that quality. Illness is present at the energetic level long before it ever manifests on the physical level.

Practicing qigong on a regular basis improves the energy so the body can improve too.

4. Going to a support group. Not all my experiences with support groups have been positive. I remember attending a support group for incest survivors. I went two times and never went back. The group culture was angry and blaming. It wasn't for me. I also tried a cancer support group that was fantastic. I did a lot of healing in the group.

Support groups can be very beneficial, but make sure you find the right group for you. Shop around for the right group. If you want to heal, you need a safe place where you can learn to trust others with your emotions. If you're in a not-so-great group, leave and look for another. You deserve the best support.

5. Walking a dog. Bob is our seven-year-old cockapoo. My spouse and I got him when I was going through chemotherapy the first time. The idea was that I'd have to get off the couch to take him for a walk. What I found was that walking loosens up my muscles and joints and lessens the pain from my osteoarthritis. I need less Advil when I walk and stay active. If you don't have a dog, you could ask to walk your neighbor's dog—especially elderly or sick neighbors. Dog walking is an enjoyable way of ensuring your own fitness as well as that of the dog. There are many benefits of walking (i.e., improvement in cardiovascular development, strengthening of muscles and bones, low blood pressure, etc.). There's also a social benefit of walking. People who go walking with their dogs are believed to be friendly and approachable by others. Walk with your pet, and you might end up making new friends as well. From the social viewpoint to the health perspective, dog walking holds many benefits. If for any reason dog walking is not possible for you, look for opportunities to pet or play with another animal, or perhaps you could rock a baby (or yourself) to sleep.

6. Appreciating nature. I wish I could put Lake Superior in my pocket to remind me of its power and energy. I can sit on the shores of the lake for hours and get totally mesmerized watching the waves. The steel blue water is soothing, and the shoreline, with its gray basalt boulders, is beautiful. I go to Lake Superior to calm my mind and refuel my spirit. All I have to do is stand on the shore, close my eyes, and feel the vast energy. It's a powerful place to meditate and talk with the Great Spirit.

One autumn night I sat on some boulders overlooking the lake. It was near midnight, and a full moon hung over the glass-like surface. The only sound came from the waves lapping the lake's edge. It was a magnificent moment, and I go back to that spot in my mind when I need to relax. I suggest that you find your own spot to go to when you need it.

Use the Attitude and Strength Steps Activity on the next page to work on your osteoarthritis or any illness that keeps you from living a life of quality and health.

ACTIVITY 7

Take Steps to Improve Your Attitude and Strength

NEVER GIVE UP

SUPPLIES: pencil or pen

For exercise my friend Shelly walks up seven flights of steep stone stairs on a street near her home. There is no doubt about it: it is a challenge to climb those steps.

One day, as she was walking up the steps, she noticed that someone had written with chalk on each landing. On the first landing was the word "JOY." The next landing read "GRATITUDE." On each landing there was a positive and uplifting word in chalk. Instead of feeling tired and fatigued, she found herself feeling energized.

Imagine yourself on a journey climbing up and down steep steps but enjoying every minute of it. Next to the steps below, write your own encouraging words. The next time you climb a set of stairs, real or metaphorical, ask yourself, "How will I feel when I reach the top?" Just as physical exercise strengthens our body and builds up our stamina, mental exercise will do the same for our mind and spirit—plus it feels really good!

Auto Accident Survival

"Rita, look out!" The red Toyota truck appeared out of nowhere going forty miles per hour. It went through the red light and slammed into the passenger side of my spouse's Mazda MX6—exactly where I was sitting. The impact threw us to the left and then to the right. The seat belts dug into our exposed necks, the windshield shattered, and the window to my right broke over me.

I floated in and out of consciousness. The objects in the ambulance seemed fuzzy and out of focus. I couldn't remember what day it was or what I'd eaten for breakfast. The pain in my body was explosive, and I worried my back was broken. I was strapped down on a gurney and instructed by an unknown face to lie very still. My gaze went left, where I found Rita sitting next to me. Her blouse was covered in blood. I lost consciousness again.

I heard glass tinkling on the floor as my clothes were removed and I was put into a shapeless, green hospital gown. A surgeon stood by, waiting to see the results of my CT scan. I was left alone for a

moment. The realization hit me. We had been
in a car accident, and I had a cracked rib; glass
shards wedged into my jaw, face, and neck; and
a concussion. Blood was found where it wasn't
supposed to be, and I heard the hospital staff
discuss emergency surgery. More tests were done to
evaluate my liver and kidneys.

The emergency room's white walls were
brilliantly lit. Green gowns and masks whirled
around me. Dr. Anderson perched over the gash in
my head, shaving the hair off so he could remove
pieces of glass and suture the wound. I could feel
the cold of the razor on my scalp. My neck and
shoulder burned from the antiseptic used to clean
the blood from the wounds on my upper body.

Rita stood next to me. I saw the red, jagged
laceration on her head. We joked about who had
more stitches and who had the hardest head. Her
swollen eyes took in the cuts, bruises, and burns on
my body. Tears ran down her cheeks, and she said
she wished she had been sitting where I had been.
We cried together and held hands.

Trauma can cause a host of physical ailments. One thing we've learned through centuries of treating trauma survivors is that those who can bring meaning to their suffering are more likely to recover and thrive.

Trauma tears your world apart and leaves you with a frightening void to fill, but you can fill your void with the right tools. In my years of experience with trauma, I've come to the realization that I need to stop myself for a moment once the trauma is over. I need to think through exactly what happened and how it happened. This is my reality check. If I can walk myself through the trauma, I may still go through denial at first, but I will be able to get over the denial faster and start healing.

When trauma or illness occurs, I find that I can do nothing at first except cry. I used to ask, "Why did this happen?" and "Why did this happen to me?" There are no answers to these questions. Trauma and illness happen. I have found, however, that the illness that may result from a trauma can be avoided. (Remember how strong the mind is? See Chapter 3.) I've turned my "why" questions into "what" questions. In other words, according to the Renewing Life program, I ask "Now that this has happened to me, what do I want to do about it?" This puts me back in control.

In all my trauma, I've found that there is always someone I can turn to help me face reality. That's why I believe family and friends are so crucial in our healing. Trauma and illness overstimulate our minds and bodies and send our nerve endings and muscles into spasms. Trauma literally fries our circuits. Having someone to talk to and cry with helps calm our nerves.

I've also learned to listen to what I consider are messages from the Great Spirit. When I listen to these messages I find I can survive trauma. For instance, two days before our car accident, Rita and I were coming back from a family event in southwestern Minnesota. I was watching the farmland go by when suddenly I heard a voice inside my head say to me, "You are going to be in an accident, but you will survive." I grasped the car seat and took several deep breaths. We made it home that day without incident.

Monday went by, and nothing happened.

Tuesday morning, a red truck came crashing into my existence. It was several days later when I remembered that voice. We indeed had been in an accident, and I had survived. So to whom did this voice belong, and where did it come from? For me the answer was simple. It was the Great Spirit warning me and comforting me all at the same time. I had no control over preventing the accident, but I had the knowledge that I would survive. That knowledge was a huge gift to me. I have probably received many warnings in my life, but I've just been too busy to hear. That's why I love my quiet time. I can allow messages from the Great Spirit to sink in, and I will hear them.

Quiet time is important. In a world filled with cell phones, tablets, and other devices, all the bells and whistles we respond to take us away from really hearing what is said to us. I admit I'm easily distracted. I hate going to restaurants where a TV is on because I usually end up watching and ignoring the people around me. I don't watch TV (unless it's an NFL game or the news) because I prefer to spend my time reading or writing. I need a quiet space for these activities, but I also need time to listen. I can avoid danger if I listen more. I don't have any statistics to back this up, but I believe that if I listen more and let myself be distracted less, I can avoid some dangers. I don't need any more trauma or illness than I've already endured. If I listen more carefully and concentrate on what I'm hearing, I can make better decisions regarding my health and safety. For example, rather than just grabbing my purse and driving to the Mall of America, I make a list of the things I need and find a parking space in a well-lighted area nearby. Before I leave my car, I look around and memorize where my car is parked. I listen for voices or noises, and if something doesn't feel right, I'm not going to leave my car. I've made these choices based on personal experience.

In 1989, I was living in South Minneapolis and working in Golden Valley, a suburb about ten miles away. One night after a meeting at work, I got into my car. It was just after ten p.m. As I started my car, I heard a voice behind me say, "Don't park in the garage." I looked behind me, but no one was there. I shook my head, but again I heard, "Don't park in the garage." The hair stood up on my neck. As I got closer to home, that voice got more demanding and insistent. I got to my neighborhood and parked my car on the street. When I came through the front door, my roommate met me looking extremely worried. "I'm so glad you didn't park in the garage," she said. I asked her what was wrong. She handed me a piece of paper. It was an announcement about several assaults on women in our neighborhood in the past several days. The attackers would hide in garages. They stole wallets and purses and, in one case, raped a woman.

I stood shaking in the entryway. If I had parked in the garage instead, what would have happened? Luckily, I had listened to that voice before I met another trauma.

The voice. Is it women's intuition, spiritual intervention, or common sense? To me it doesn't matter. It's a voice that warns me about possible problems and how I can avoid them. We hear and see signs all the time, but most of us just ignore them. Imagine the trouble we could avoid if we listened for messages or looked for signs.

I know that admitting to hearing voices makes me sound a bit unhinged. That's why I like to say the Great Spirit is sending me a message. To me, not listening to the message is foolish—and dangerous.

Tools to Cope with Trauma from Accidents

Below are tools that helped me recover from the car accident.

1. Quiet time. This fantastic tool isn't easy to use because of all the distractions in our lives. But try this: Find a quiet room in your house or at a library, or even sit in your car. Shut your eyes for a minute (if you're in your car, please put it in "park" before closing your eyes). Take a couple of deep breaths, and try to exhale all of your conscious thoughts. That's right: exhale the worries about your chil-

dren and their report cards, exhale your work schedule tomorrow, and exhale what you're going to be making for dinner tonight. Just breathe, and let your mind float. If you find you can't stay focused, try visualizing the flame of a candle or ocean waves rolling in on a sandy beach. Tell yourself that you are ready to hear any messages that are being sent to you. Keep taking deep breaths if you find yourself being distracted. Sometimes the messages are right there, and sometimes they aren't. Keep trying whenever you can make a moment of quiet time.

2. Listening. I've trained myself how to listen better. It's not that I don't want to listen; it's just that when I hear something, I'm often thinking about my response. Now I try to shut down the need to respond and focus on listening. Here are a few suggestions to improve your listening ability while driving:

- Eliminate distractions while driving. Don't talk or text on your phone while driving.
- Listen for emergency vehicles' sirens.
- If a passenger gets in your car and immediately wants to talk about a recent trauma or crisis, don't start the car. Having a serious conversation while driving can lead to an accident.
- Use nonverbal skills. To let a family member or friend know you're listening while you're driving, try simply nodding or smiling. Your facial expressions can be comforting.

3. Applying ice. You think I'm kidding, right? Wrong. Applying ice to bruises, swollen joints, and broken limbs is a great tool to take away pain and reduce the inflammation from injuries. While you're applying ice, why don't you go back to number 1, and take some quiet time for yourself. This tool works great on headaches, too.

4. Insurance. I'm not talking about car insurance here. I'm talking about wearing your seat belt whenever you travel. If Rita and I had not had our seat belts on the day of our car accident, we both would have gone through the windshield. Save your life and reduce your injuries by wearing a seat belt in all moving vehicles.

5. Talking. With all the comments I've made about listening, you also need to talk about your accident to loved ones and friends. Talking is cathartic: it will release your fears and may reduce the number of nightmares you experience. If nightmares persist, you may want to see a therapist for further help. So start talking, and start healing.

ACTIVITY 8

Put Premium Fuel in Your Body

SUPPLIES: pencil or pen, paper

What do you think about when you drive in your car? Are you burdened by your to-do list? Do you focus on your worries? Are you loaded down with baggage? Do you get cranky with other drivers?

Your body can be like a car that is overburdened, unmaintained, and filled with bad fuel. What if you put premium fuel in your car—that is, in your body? In other words, what if you fuel yourself with empowering thoughts? What if you said things like this? "What a wonderful day this is! I intend to have a positive and productive day. My interactions with people will be happy and hopeful. My appointment with my doctor will go well. I love myself. I love and bless everyone I meet."

List some of your typical thoughts here:

_____
_____
_____
_____

Write some premium fuel thoughts for your body here:

_____
_____
_____
_____

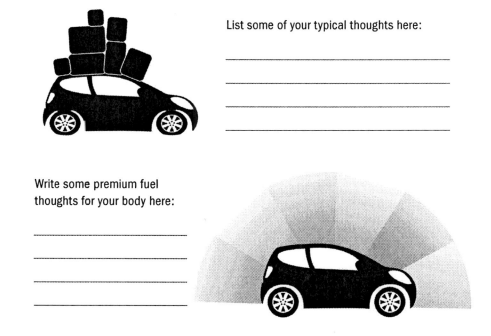

Illness as Trauma

It's not what happens but how you think about what happens that will shape your future.
—**Anonymous**

Trauma can turn into illness if the trauma is not dealt with in a timely and appropriate manner. What happens when illness develops without a preceding trauma? The effects of chronic or life-threatening illness run parallel to trauma.

In her book *Invisible Heroes: Survivors of Trauma and How They Heal*, Belleruth Naparstek writes, "The most common physical complaints that immediately follow a chronic or life-threatening illness experience are restlessness, hypervigilance, problems with falling asleep or staying asleep, generalized anxiety, inability to relax, shallow breathing, fatigue, and an exaggerated startle response at sudden noises and/or unexpected touch. A goodly number of people also experience headaches, backaches, temporomandibular joint (TMJ), various skin complaints such as itching and rashes, and unintentional weight loss."

According to anthropologist Dennis O'Neil, typical causes of illness accepted in naturalistic medical systems include:

1. organic breakdown or deterioration (e.g., tooth decay, heart failure, senility)
2. obstruction (e.g., kidney stones, arterial blockage due to plaque build-up)
3. injury (e.g., broken bones, bullet wounds)
4. imbalance (e.g., too much or too little of specific hormones and salts in the blood)
5. malnutrition (e.g., too much or too little food, not enough proteins, vitamins, or minerals)
6. parasites (e.g., bacteria, viruses, amoebas, worms)

To get sick, all you have to do is slide your hand along a railing at a school, fitness center, or shopping mall and touch your hands to your eyes, nose, or mouth. Your chances of picking up harmful microbes increase, and if you have the type of system that can't resist bacteria or viruses, you're sure to end up with a whopping cold or sinus infection. These can lead to bronchitis and pneumonia. Your best defense is to frequently wash your hands with soap and warm water.

How can our emotions affect our health?

Did you know that our bodies respond to the way we think, feel, and act? Called the "mind-body connection," our bodies signal something isn't right through stress and anxiety. High blood pressure or a stomach ulcer can develop after a stressful event, such as the death of a loved one. The following may be physical signs that your emotional health is out of balance:

Back pain
High blood pressure
Sexual problems
Change in appetite
Insomnia (trouble sleeping)

Shortness of breath
Chest pain
Lightheadedness
Stiff neck
Constipation or diarrhea
Palpitations (the feeling that your heart is racing)
Sweating
Dry mouth
Shortness of breath
Upset stomach
Extreme tiredness
Weight gain or loss
General aches and pains
Headaches

Hundreds of studies report that poor emotional health can weaken your body's immune system. You're more likely to get colds and other infections during emotionally difficult times. When you feel stressed, anxious, or upset, taking care of your health may decrease. Activities like exercising, eating nutritious foods, or taking medicine that your doctor prescribes become harder to do. Signs of poor emotional health include abuse of alcohol, tobacco, or other drugs.

I know that trauma weakened my immune system, although I also know that my gene pool is unhealthy. My mother died from breast cancer, but she also had a severe heart condition. In 1986 she had a quadruple bypass, which resulted in a stroke.

Mom blamed herself for the fact that my brother and I developed insulin-dependent diabetes (Type 1). My maternal grandmother was thirty-six-years old when she died from diabetes, and my mom believed she passed her diabetes genes to us. When my family went through genetic counseling at the University of Minnesota, researchers found that my father also carried the gene for diabetes. This helped my mother considerably because she could share the blame. (Of course, no one can be blamed for their genetic inheritance.)

My father, on the other hand, was an amazing man when it came to illnesses. He just didn't get sick. His unhealthy expressions of anger helped facilitate relative good health. The sickness he did suffer was directly related to his addiction to alcohol, including stomachaches, headaches, and sinus infections. His symptoms got worse from the amount of alcohol he consumed. To our surprise, he lived to be ninety-three years old and died from pneumonia.

There are many reasons we get sick. Our DNA makeup is what it is. Illness, however, can be healed just like trauma. Though a cure may not yet be in existence for diabetes, cancer, or AIDS, a balance among the mind, body, and spirit can reduce the long-term effects of illness. In the right frame of mind, you can overcome huge obstacles, tackle challenges, and beat big odds.

I've lived with diabetes for forty-one years and have had few complications. I had to have the lenses in my eyes replaced with manufactured ones as a result of cataracts (which are associated with diabetes), but I've pretty much escaped many of the ugly side effects. I've not been hospitalized for high blood sugar since 1975. Good adherence to diet, exercise, and medication help to hold off the more problematic side effects, like retinopathy and neuropathy—numbness of the fingers or feet).

If you've been recently diagnosed with a chronic or life-threatening illness, remember that you didn't deserve it. Luckily, medical research has improved the treatments for hundreds of illnesses. The best thing you can do is have a very open and deep conversation with your doctor. Ask questions about different treatment plans. Find out the statistics of what works and what doesn't. Your endocrinologist, rheumatologist, or oncologist is a specialist in your illness and should have a vast amount of knowledge to share with you.

Don't be afraid to ask, and don't feel that you're bothering your doctor. Their job is to help you understand your illness, the treatment, the side effects, and the outcome. It's your job to get answers you can understand. If you have a doctor who doesn't communicate well, try another doctor if you can.

After my first surgery for colon cancer, the doctor who performed my surgery came in to see me. I started to ask a lot of questions. His response was, "Patience is a virtue." In other words, he shamed me for wanting to know about colon cancer. I dropped him like a hot rock and went on to find the most wonderful oncologist and general surgeon. I get my questions answered now without having to feel shamed. You can do the same.

Chronic and life-threatening illnesses come with a boatload of emotions. If you try to sidestep your feelings, they'll just come back to slap you in the face. Be honest with yourself in coping with your illness. I do lots of research to help me understand the illness and the accompanying emotional side effects. I want to know what I'm up against rather than let fear take over. Experiencing feelings of fear is a natural part of illness and trauma, but fear can fuel depression and anxiety, and it grows from unfounded worries and lack of information. When you acknowledge your fear, you are also strengthening your immune system. Learn the facts about your illness, and listen to your health care provider's recommendations. Knowledge is powerful and can reduce your fear.

Tools on Living with a Chronic or Life-Threatening Illness

The following tools can help you cope with chronic or life-threatening illness.

1. Get educated. Ask a lot of questions and get answers that you understand. Learn everything you can about your illness, even the history of its fascinating discovery. The more you know, the smaller the fear becomes. Find out what you can do and what you can't do.

2. Take an assertive stance on your diagnosis. For example, express your needs with "I" statements such as "I need your help to understand my diagnosis because this news frightens me. Please give me more details." Ask questions about what effects the treatment(s) will have on you so you can be prepared.

3. Ask to see your CT and PET scans. This visualization will help you see the spot where the illness/disease is and see the condition it is in. (During my colonoscopy, I saw on the monitor the two feet of diseased colon. It was scary looking, but it helped me get through the denial stage quickly.)

4. Handle your diagnosis and treatment in small amounts. This will lower your fear of the unknown.

5. Follow your doctor's treatment plan. If you don't like it, ask about alternative options.

6. Be aware that your illness will change your emotions, your relationships, and, ultimately, your life. Be prepared, and take in the news with a mix of seriousness and humor.

7. Make a goal every day. Then make a goal for several months ahead. This provides the motivation you need to keep going.

8. Know your resources. Nearly every chronic and life-threatening illness has a professional association that can provide information and referral services. Medical websites can give you information on where to get help, support groups, and alternative therapies.

9. Get support. Friends and family may help you, but if you need more intensive support, contact a therapist who specializes in your disease. Most doctors' offices have a list of resources for you.

10. Look at your finances. Illnesses are costly even if you have insurance. You may be surprised by the amount of deductibles and

out-of-pocket expenses you have to pay. Seek financial advice before you let worry make you even more ill.

11. Talk to your boss or employer about your illness. You may have to take additional time off or even a medical leave. Check into your benefits plan so you can make the right choices regarding your treatment.

12. Find a worthwhile job if you're unemployed. Your illness will change your views on life and your views on what you do. If a job offer makes your heart beat faster, then take a serious look at it.

13. Eat right. Illnesses can deplete your body of healthy nutrients. Make sure you're getting enough of the foods that increase your red blood cells.

14. Find time to relax or go on a vacation. Living with a chronic or life-threatening illness is draining. Refuel your spirit with some time away from your illness if you can. Many studies show that a relaxed state can reduce side effects and increase your immune system.

15. Read stories about people who have your illness and are surviving. Their examples will help you see that a chronic illness doesn't mean a death sentence.

16. Make a will. I found this to be extremely helpful "just in case." It took a lot of worry off my plate. People may see this as a morbid activity on your part, but once you have this done, you'll have wonderful peace of mind.

And remember to look over all the tools I've listed in this book, and create your own tool kit. Miracles do happen, but you need to make sure your body, mind, and spirit are balanced no matter what. You want to be in the best condition when the cure is discovered.

ACTIVITY 9

Heal Your Heart Quadrants

NEVER GIVE UP

SUPPLIES: colored pencils or pens or pastels or chalk, paper

On the next page is an image of a heart divided into four quadrants:

Quadrant 1: Hopeful Heart
Quadrant 2: Worried Heart
Quadrant 3: Happy Heart
Quadrant 4: Emotion of Choice
(Write in an emotion.)

Using lines, shapes, and colors, draw an image in each quadrant that represents the emotions above.

Start by comparing quadrants 1 and 2, and reflect on these questions:

➤ Why did you choose the colors you did?
➤ Why did you choose the lines and shapes you did?
➤ What colors and shapes in your environment affect you? (Your environment includes your home, your work setting, and any other places you may go, including clinic or hospital, stores, friends' homes, and so forth.)
➤ What color best resonates with you personally and why?

Now compare quadrants 3 and 4, and reflect on the same questions.

QUADRANT 1
Hopeful Heart

QUADRANT 2
Worried Heart

QUADRANT 3
Happy Heart

QUADRANT 4
Emotion of Choice

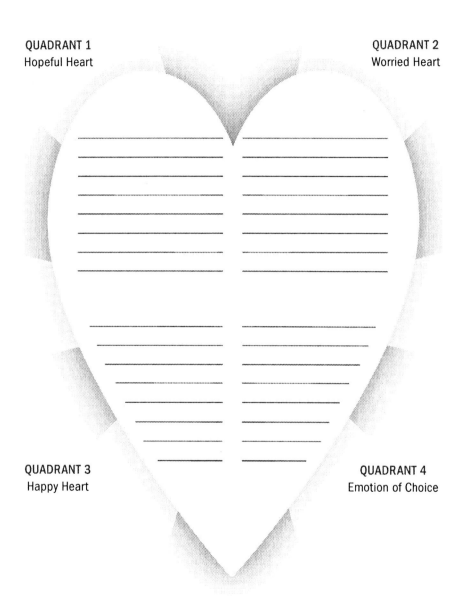

Diabetes: It's Not Just About Sugar

Being diagnosed with a chronic or life-threatening illness is devastating.

I was fifteen years old when I joined my junior high school track and basketball teams, but after one month, I started to feel sick. I was losing weight at the same time that I was depleting my family's food cupboards. I was always thirsty. I drank gallons of water and soda pop, but the thirst never went away. In three days I lost nine pounds. Then I started having to go to the bathroom multiple times during the day. I was also getting up three times during the night to urinate. By day four I was scared. I talked to my mom. Because her mother had diabetes, Mom knew the signs and symptoms. She immediately took me to the doctor. The next day I was hospitalized. I was diagnosed with insulin-dependent diabetes (Type 1).

In the hospital, I had to learn how to test my urine for sugar (when I was diagnosed there were only urine tests available to detect the amount of sugar in my body), how to give myself insulin injections, how to eat right, and how to change my life to accommodate my diabetes.

What surprised me most was that I had so many friends tell me that they wouldn't be able to take insulin injections. I found this to be a strange comment, because if you knew you'd die if you didn't take insulin, wouldn't you find the courage? I know I did. It wasn't a difficult choice for me—take the injections and live, or don't take the injections and die.

Emotionally, I felt totally abnormal from my friends and siblings. My body changed right before my very eyes. I lost weight, and I looked tired all the time. I went through the motions of trying to stay on my treatment plan, but I hated it. I ended up going to the hospital twice because I rebelled: I didn't watch what I ate, I wasn't testing my urine, and my blood sugars went berserk.

There were two guys in my high school class who also had diabetes, but it was hard for me to go to them for comfort. Sure, we talked about what a bummer it was to have diabetes, but we never talked about our anger and fear. I think that first year I was in total shock and denial. I saw myself as damaged, much like the feelings I had had so many other times. The only thing that kept me going was that I learned (on a subconscious level) that if I ended up in the hospital, my dad wouldn't come to visit. I don't know why, but he hated hospitals. So in my subconscious, if I needed to get away from my dad, I'd elevate my blood sugars, get sick, and end up in the hospital, where I would be safe. I learned very quickly how to use my diabetes to find safety in a frightening environment.

When my brother was diagnosed three years after I was, I got angry and traumatized all over again. Wasn't it enough to have one kid in the family with diabetes? Why did he have to go through what I did? Didn't we have enough to face with people constantly reminding us not to eat certain foods? Then there were all the stories of how people died from diabetes because they didn't take care of themselves. None of this made sense to me; it seemed so unfair. I am one year older than my brother, and, as his older sister, I felt responsible for his diagnosis. I know now that this was ridiculous thinking. I had no responsibility for his illness, but I was eighteen years old and trying to make sense out of my world.

Tools for Living with Diabetes

The following tools have helped me live with diabetes for forty years. Some of these tools have been included in previous chapters, but here I give you more information as to how these tools can specifically help with diabetes.

1. Medication. I take insulin every day because my pancreas doesn't secrete insulin on its own. The simple truth is that I need insulin to live just like millions of other people. Whether you take insulin or a pill to help your pancreas secrete more insulin, don't mess around with your medication. Just take it. If you don't take enough, you'll get sick fast.

I love being on an insulin pump. I find the pump to be really manageable, and it helps balance my blood sugars better. At first the idea of being tethered to a pump didn't thrill me, but after a few weeks, when I saw my blood sugars balance out, I became an insulin pump wearer for good. Insulin pumps have become much smaller since they were first invented, and they have many different functions. It's like wearing a computer. (Actually, it is a computer.) I can change my insulin profiles depending on what I'm doing. For instance, while going through chemotherapy, I had an insulin profile set up where I got more insulin per hour because of the steroids and other IV meds that increased my blood sugar level. After the chemo drugs were finished for the week, I just went back to my normal insulin profile. It worked really well. If you're interested in an insulin pump, talk to your endocrinologist for their recommendation. You can also search online or contact the American Diabetes Association for a list of pump manufacturers in your area.

2. Eating right. I love eating, and yet I hate eating. It's a tough position to be in when you have diabetes. Food is so important in the maintenance of balanced blood sugars. Sure, I like food, but not when I have to eat because my blood sugar is low. For instance, I've made the mistake many times where I take too much insulin before a meal. I'll eat my meal and feel very content. Then my blood sugar starts falling because I took too much insulin, which results in having to eat more food when I'm already full. Or I feel low, and I still have to eat to make sure my blood sugars don't dip more. That's why it's so important to regularly check your blood sugar levels. You may *think* your blood sugar is okay until you test it and find out that you're high or low.

3. Exercise. When I was growing up, I loved to run and play. I played kickball and basketball. I'd throw the football around with my brothers and sisters. My mother would take us swimming as a family. We'd go hiking and on walks. We were always moving. In my fifties, I have a harder time being motivated to exercise. I have a treadmill that I use every other day. I've tried to stay consistent with my exercise, but it doesn't happen as easily as it did when I was younger. I know I need to exercise for my overall health and my blood sugar maintenance. Whether I like it or not, I exercise. Having a dog helps because I have to walk him every day. He's a great motivator because he'll stand by the door and whine until I put on my walking shoes and open the door.

Walking is my favorite way to exercise because I can think about things while I'm walking. It has not only a physical benefit but an emotional one as well. I enjoy being outside to observe the seasons. Here in Minnesota we get four definite seasons (though winter seems to dominate), and I like watching the transition from season to season. I also enjoy golfing. With my game the way it is, I get a lot of exercise swinging those clubs. Find an exercise routine that meets your lifestyle and makes you feel good.

4. Your diabetes specialist. My diabetes specialist and his staff are wonderful. I've been seeing them for thirty years. They know my medical history and how I treat my diabetes. They know I'm a team player when it comes to handling my diabetes. They were especially valuable to me when I was going through chemotherapy. My blood sugars were in the 300s and 400s (normal is between 80 to 120 milligrams per deciliter). With the chemotherapy and medications I was on, I got confused about my diabetes management. I needed help even though I'd been managing my diabetes for years. I went in for special visits to review my insulin requirements and how to manage my diabetes when I was nauseated or fatigued from the chemotherapy. I also relied on my diabetes specialist when I had sleep apnea surgery and I couldn't eat for the first few weeks while I mended. My diabetes team is a real gift in helping me maintain my health.

I also don't miss my appointments with my endocrinologist or ophthalmologist. My diabetes specialist and my ophthalmologist work together to make sure my eyes are in good health. I don't want to lose my vision, and I know that blood glucose control is important in this area. So, see your health care team at least every six months. If something comes up, call your doctor right away—the faster you get help, the faster you can get the right treatment.

5. Attitude. Diabetes is a challenging disease. There are many variables you need to watch while maintaining balanced blood sugars. It takes a lot of work and can become difficult at times. But you are not your disease. Maintaining a positive attitude toward your diabetes and your diabetes control will help you get through the tough times. When I was diagnosed, my whole life was consumed with having diabetes. As time went on, I found that my diabetes was easier to handle on both a physical and an emotional level. Sure, I tested the limits of my eating and my insulin dosages because I was rebellious. I didn't want to have diabetes, but nothing I can do will

take it away. The best thing I can do for myself is to treat diabetes like everything else in my life. I need to be conscious of the setbacks and maintain my eating and exercising. When I'm feeling depressed, I need to take extra time to make sure my blood sugars are within the normal level. If they are low or high and I don't feel well, this only makes me more depressed. I don't want to start that ugly cycle, so I do what I can to help my blood sugars and my mood. Sometimes I just yell, "I hate diabetes!" It takes the edge off, and I can continue on. Try it. It's okay to yell (except if you're at the opera).

ACTIVITY 10

Make Healthy Choices at the Salad Bar

SUPPLIES: pens, paper

You're in the mood for a healthy, delicious salad. You can pick anything you want—any food from any culture is possible. Select at least eight ingredients. List all the ingredients, and for each one, list one of your personal strengths.

Your strengths, just like healthy foods, bring energy and vitality to your mind, body, and spirit. You can come up with at least eight strengths!

Here are some examples:

- Salad greens
- Tomato
- Cucumber
- Pear slices

- Cheerfulness
- Calm under pressure
- Strong-willed
- Energetic

YOUR INGREDIENTS	YOUR STRENGTHS
➤	➤
➤	➤
➤	➤
➤	➤
➤	➤
➤	➤

Sleep Apnea: When You Can't Breathe When You Sleep

It's 1:13 a.m.   *I'm awake and in horrible pain.*
It's 1:52 a.m.   *My throat is on fire.*
It's 2:15 a.m.   *I took some more pain medication.*
It's 2:23 a.m.   *I'm crying my eyes out.*
It's 2:30 a.m.   *I wonder why I developed sleep apnea.*
It's 3:08 a.m.   *I'm praying I'll pass out from the pain.*
It's 3:15 a.m.   *The pain medication is finally working.*
It's 3: 48 a.m.   *Did I develop sleep apnea because I wouldn't talk about the abuse I suffered?*
It's 4:02 a.m.   *I'm feeling sleepy.*
It's 4:37 a.m.   *I just woke up from a nightmare.*
It's 4:55 a.m.   *What do I need to do to stop all these medical conditions from developing? (No answer.)*
It's 5:45 a.m.   *Can I take some more pain medication? No.*
It's 6:10 a.m.   *I've got to do something about this.*
It's 6:11 a.m.   *I need to write a book about the abuse.*

When you suffer from sleep apnea, sleep becomes a nightly battle. You toss and turn. Your body jolts you awake. You snore. You may experience nightmares. You're restless and edgy. You wake up tired. You spend your day trying not to fall asleep. You have no energy to do anything. You wonder what's wrong. You go to your doctor. Your doctor recommends that you see a sleep specialist. You worry about your treatment options.

If you have sleep apnea, you know what it is and how awful it can be. For those not familiar with sleep apnea, let me give a brief introduction to it. According to the American Sleep Apnea Association:

> Sleep apnea is an involuntary cessation of breathing that occurs while the patient is asleep. There are three types of sleep apnea: obstructive, central, and mixed. Of the three, obstructive sleep apnea . . . is the most common. Despite the difference in the root cause of each type, in all three, people with untreated sleep apnea stop breathing repeatedly during their sleep, sometimes hundreds of times during the night and often for a minute or longer. In most cases the sleeper is unaware of these breath stoppages because they don't trigger a full awakening.

Sleep apnea is as common as adult diabetes and affects more than twelve million Americans, according to the National Institutes of Health. Risk factors include being male, overweight, and over the age of forty, but sleep apnea can strike anyone at any age, even children. Because of the lack of awareness by the public and health care professionals, the vast majority remain undiagnosed despite the fact that this serious disorder can have significant consequences. Untreated sleep apnea can cause high blood pressure and other cardiovascular diseases, memory problems, weight gain, impotency, and headaches. Fortunately, sleep apnea can be diagnosed and treated. Several treatment options exist, and research into additional options continues.

I don't know when I started developing sleep apnea. I do know that my quality of life was going down the drain fast. I was always so tired that I could hardly make it through the day. I had to drink caffeinated beverages at lunch so I wouldn't fall asleep at my desk in the afternoons. Then I'd go home, have dinner, and sleep on the couch until it was time to go to bed. During the night, I'd wake up so frequently that I never dreamed, so I knew I was never getting into the healthy Rapid Eye Movement (REM) stage of sleep.

After months and months of sleepless nights, I went in to see my primary physician. I told her about being so tired. She asked me to open my mouth. "Okay," she said, "your throat is abnormally narrow. Do you snore?" I nodded. She said, "I'm going to send you to a sleep clinic to have a test done. I think you've got sleep apnea."

I was stunned. The only thing I knew about sleep apnea was that you could fall asleep while you were driving. That was just too scary for me. I followed my physician's recommendation and went to a sleep clinic.

The test results showed that I stopped breathing seventy times per hour. Sleep apnea experts say these breathing lapses can happen four hundred times every night. My brain and body would jolt me awake so that I would continue breathing. No wonder I never felt refreshed after sleeping.

Sleep apnea occurs when there isn't enough air to fill your lungs during sleep. Your throat muscles normally keep your throat open so air can flow into your lungs. With obstructive sleep apnea, the throat muscles collapse and close, causing pauses in your breathing. Some of the factors that cause apnea are the following:

- the oxygen in your blood drops
- your throat muscles and tongue relax too much
- you're overweight
- your tonsils and adenoids are enlarged

- your head and neck bone structure are too small and narrow
- your breathing is hard and noisy (snoring)

So my throat was abnormally narrow, I snored, and I was overweight. Now that I knew what sleep apnea was and what caused it, I wanted to know what types of treatments were available.

Unfortunately, there are no medicines for the treatment of sleep apnea. People with moderate or severe sleep apnea need treatment, such as Continuous Positive Airway Pressure (CPAP), which is the most common treatment for sleep apnea. Usually a technician comes to your home to bring the CPAP equipment. The technician will set up the CPAP machine and make adjustments based on your doctor's orders. You wear a mask over your nose and mouth during sleep. The mask blows air into your throat at a pressure level that is right for you. The increased airway pressure keeps your throat open while you sleep. The air pressure is adjusted so you get enough to stop your airways from briefly getting too small during sleep.

Treating sleep apnea may help you stop snoring, but that does not mean you no longer have sleep apnea or you can stop using CPAP. Sleep apnea will return if CPAP is stopped or if it is not used correctly.

People with severe sleep apnea symptoms generally feel much better once they begin treatment with CPAP, but it didn't work for me. I had to have surgery.

Uvulopalatopharyngoplasty (UPPP) is a surgery that removes the tonsils, uvula (the tissue that hangs from the middle of the back of the roof of the mouth), and part of your soft palate (the roof of your mouth in the back of your throat). This surgery is only effective for some people with sleep apnea.

I went to an ear, nose, and throat (ENT) specialist, and a month later I was in surgery having a UPPP. For six very long weeks I was in a lot of pain. Even heavy-duty narcotics couldn't take away the pain. Taking in a breath of air even hurt. To swallow was a nightmare.

Luckily for me, the surgery worked (along with repairing my deviated septum and removing my adenoids and tonsils). I had a really low, sexy voice for a month, but as my throat healed I had no remaining effects. I could sleep again, and I had more energy than I'd had in over five years. I was ecstatic.

Tools for Coping with Sleep Apnea

When you repair something in your house, you know that some tools are better than others. You're not going to use a screwdriver to pound a nail into a wall. (You could use the screwdriver's handle, but it wouldn't be as effective as a hammer.) So different tools are needed for different situations. When it comes to sleep apnea, here are the tools I found and now keep in my tool kit:

1. Health care team. A knowledgeable surgeon gave me the diagnosis and treatment options for all my sleep apnea symptoms. Because he held the knowledge of the human body that I don't, I looked to him to recommend the appropriate course of action. I asked him what option he recommended. "If you were in my place, what would you choose?" I've found that this question helps my health care team focus on the human side of treatment. I've learned that they don't recommend a procedure if they themselves would not do it. This question also makes them see me as a real person, not just a patient number. When I asked my ENT specialist if he had my narrow throat and enlarged tonsils and adenoids, would he have the surgery, he said yes.

2. Treatment options. With sleep apnea, not everyone needs to have surgery. Many people find help using a CPAP machine. Others may need a special mouthpiece. All of us, however, need to make some lifestyle changes, such as watching what we eat and maintain-

ing a healthy weight. I tried the CPAP for a month, but it didn't give me the type of results I hoped to have. Trust me, I didn't want to have surgery, so I prayed that the CPAP would work. When it didn't, I was so discouraged. I went online to see what people were saying about the surgery. Many of the people who had the surgery were very positive about their experience, though they did admit to how painful it was. There were also those the surgery didn't help and they had gone through awful pain for nothing. I did more research and took both sides into consideration before I decided to have surgery.

3. Reading. I did a lot of research on sleep apnea before I went into surgery. I was stunned to find out I had sleep apnea, and I was feeling like a total loser again. Why me? Why do I have to have this? I found out that sleep apnea affects a lot of people—not just me. I learned what it was and what caused it. I learned how it was treated and what the success rates were for each treatment option. Because I learned as much as I could about sleep apnea, I felt more confident about the situation. Though my treatment option came down to surgery, I still felt I was in control of the decision to have surgery. I also knew that I could control my healing and outcome. It was a wise decision on my part because surgery did help and I can sleep again.

4. Sleep. I used sleep as an escape. I didn't use drugs or alcohol. My choice to escape was to take a nap. I had to change my view of sleep to realize that sleep is necessary to heal, and in fact, sleep *is* healing. When I was recovering from cancer, I complained to my oncologist that I was always sleeping. He told me that sleeping is a good thing because it promotes healing and quickens the healing time. He told me not to feel guilty about sleeping because my body needed it just as it needed the chemo drugs. Since then I no longer view sleeping as a bad thing. I know when I'm using sleep to escape, and I know when I use sleep to heal. They're two very different situations, and I'm glad I learned the difference.

According to the Division of Sleep Medicine at Harvard Medical School, sleep is critical for things like your immune system and your memory. In fact, if you don't get adequate sleep, you may find your "judgment, mood, [and] ability to learn and retain information" are impaired. Over the long term, chronic sleep deprivation "may lead to a host of health problems including obesity, diabetes, cardiovascular disease, and even early mortality."

A special note to hospital staff:
After having major surgery, patients need adequate periods of uninterrupted sleep. During my stays in the hospital, the staff woke me four times during the night. At eleven p.m., staff woke me to see if I was having trouble sleeping; at one a.m., they came into my room to ask me if I needed more pain medication; at three a.m., they came in to test my blood sugar; at six a.m. they'd test my blood sugar again because breakfast had arrived.

All hospital staff should work to reduce interruptions and noise, relieve patients' anxieties, and help them sleep. Nothing can heal the body and mind like uninterrupted sleep.

ACTIVITY 11

Change Your Batteries for Better Sleep

SUPPLIES: a cool, dark room; blanket; pillow; bed

Are you tired of being tired? It's time to change your batteries! Which set of batteries out of the three below do you think you have right now? How can you make sure you have the batteries that will give you optimal sleep?

The contributing factors listed with the following three batteries can help you decide if you need to change your batteries.

SEVERE LACK OF SLEEP BATTERY

- ➤ exercising right before bedtime
- ➤ eating heavy foods right before bedtime
- ➤ screen time (TV, computer, tablet, etc.) right before bedtime
- ➤ feeling angry or fearful and not being able to express it
- ➤ sleeping in a too-warm room
- ➤ having sleep interrupted several times during the night
- ➤ reviewing stressful events that happened during the day while trying to go to sleep

ADEQUATE SLEEP BATTERY

- taking a warm bath before bed
- avoiding caffeine and alcohol before sleep
- quitting smoking
- visualizing a peaceful, restful place
- listening to soft music
- wearing a sleep mask
- doing light reading
- getting out of bed and distracting yourself temporarily
- eliminating loud noises

OPTIMAL SLEEP HABITS BATTERY

- getting eight to ten hours of solid sleep each night
- breathing deeply
- relaxing the muscles in the neck and shoulders
- thinking of something very calming
- knowing your ideal sleep conditions
- counting your blessings
- meditating
- feeling love and acceptance

Cancer: A Life Changer

Before I turned fifty, many people told me I would love this time of my life. "Life," they said, "will be more fulfilling and worthwhile." When my position at the company I worked for was eliminated in January 2007, ten days before my fiftieth birthday, things weren't turning out to be so wonderful. I was now unemployed. I was angry and sad; once again, I felt my self-confidence draining.

February went by, and I was still unemployed and feeling depressed.

In my March appointment with my urologist, he decided to take an x-ray of my pelvis and abdomen. The x-rays showed a spot on my liver, and my urologist referred me to a surgeon. The surgeon recommended that I have a colonoscopy. He didn't like the look of the spot.

On March 22, 2007, I went in to have my first colonoscopy. During the procedure, I saw bright red tissue on the monitor that quickly turned to a pale pink, deep red, and finally to black. The test was stopped. Four hours later I was in surgery, having two feet of my colon removed.

I was diagnosed with stage 4 colon cancer. The cancer had spread to my lymph nodes and liver. If I didn't have more surgery and chemotherapy, I would die.

Life tossed my spouse and me on our heads. How could this have happened? Why us? Didn't we have enough to deal with? How were we going to pay the medical bills? Why was my body betraying me again? The questions kept coming, but there were no answers.

I spent fourteen days in the hospital trying to come to grips with cancer. I had a huge incision in my stomach, and I was in a lot of pain. I went home barely able to walk. Ten days later, my surgeon recommended a PET scan to see how the colon reconstruction looked. After the PET scan, I started feeling sick. I couldn't put my finger on what the problem was and thought maybe I had just eaten too much for lunch. Around four p.m., the surgeon's office called to inform me that I had developed an abscess at the surgical site and I needed to go to the hospital the next day to have it drained. The next day? Why wasn't I told to come into the ER right there and then? Again no answers. My fears took root and spread like fire.

Terror. My thoughts centered on the abscess bursting open and spreading who-knows-what-yucky-stuff throughout my body. When I was admitted into the hospital the next day, the surgeon told me that my abscess was the size of a volleyball. I was prepped for a drain. There would be no sedative; the surgical team needed me awake. The pain was severe, but I tried not to scream. It felt as if twenty bees were buzzing and stinging my lower abdomen. When the drain was finally inserted and sealed, I was given pain medication.

I spent another twelve days in the hospital. When the drain was removed, a larger one was put in. During the surgery, I also got an ileostomy, which involves bringing the ileum (the last portion of the small intestine) to the abdominal surface. When waste matter reaches the ileum, it is liquid, so an appliance is needed to collect it. In other words, I had a bag hanging from my stomach collecting my waste. Though I was told that the ileostomy was temporary (my colon needed about six months to heal completely), I was frightened. The opening on my abdomen looked so raw, and the adhesive that held the bag in place irritated my skin. Into the second month I met a friend for dinner, and—horror of horrors—my bag leaked. I was humiliated. (Imagine the smell. Okay, don't imagine the smell.)

Just the word "cancer" elicits fear and dread. There are many types of cancer, but we often think of it as a death sentence. My mother died from breast cancer, so I thought that's the type of cancer I eventually would be diagnosed with. My sisters felt the same way. When I was diagnosed with colon cancer, it shook the family foundation.

How could I have gotten colon cancer? Why me? My body and mind spiraled into a grotesque swirl. How could I live? What if I die? Who would look after Rita? How would she survive? "Why" questions fueled my fear and plagued my thoughts. I would lay awake in the dark nights wondering how I'd fight this awful, terrible monster. Luckily for me, the dark nights began to ebb, and I started to deal with my fears.

Upon hearing that I was diagnosed with cancer, a wonderful friend of ours told Rita about a website that could help us communicate with our friends and family. The CaringBridge website was a blessing. Rita was able to post daily medical updates, so our friends and family could stay in the know. They could also send us messages. CaringBridge became a lifeline to the people who mattered so much to us.

Here are a couple of updates Rita put on the site early in my diagnosis:

> Sunday, March 25, 2007
> Hello All,
> At this point I don't know who knows what so I thought I'd send a broadcast email to everyone I can think of to make sure the word is spread. Feel free to pass the message along to others who might want to know.

Thursday Alex went in for her 50-year colonoscopy and they discovered a "mass" in her colon that looks very suspicious. As luck would have it, the surgeon had an opening in his schedule and she went in for a sigmoid colon resection (I hope I got that right) later that day. It was a bit of a whirlwind getting that accomplished but it was a good thing because she didn't have to go home and stew about it for a week and she didn't have to go through the prep again. Those of you who've done the "cleaning out" process will appreciate that!

They took out approximately two feet of her colon and sewed the two sides back together. They sent it off to the lab to get checked and we don't have the results yet but based on what the doctor is saying it looks very much like cancer. If it is, but has not gotten into her lymph nodes, she'll need no further treatment. If they find anything suspicious in the lymph nodes, she'll need some additional treatment but we just don't know at this point. The lab results are supposed to be back Monday or Tuesday.

Alex is currently recovering from surgery at North Memorial Hospital in room 402. She is still on IV and oxygen and is very, very tired but each day she makes great progress. Today she's off the morphine drip and she's taken a few walks up and down the hall with her IV pole. She had a few visitors today and managed to sit in the chair for a couple of them. She's still snoozing a lot so if you stop by to visit, don't be surprised if she falls asleep on you.

The doctor today said she may go home on Tuesday but nothing definite yet. It depends on when she gets to solid food, gets off the oxygen, etc. I'm keeping my fingers crossed it's not any later than Tuesday because I know she'll sleep so much better at home. The hospital is a terrible place to be when you don't feel well—especially when you're in a semi-private room and your roommate is noisy! The staff is really great, though, and the doctor who's been stopping by is really nice and seems very pleased with the progress Alex is making.

> I want to thank everyone who has stopped by or called or sent flowers or just sent good wishes. We're very lucky to have such wonderful friends and family. Keep those prayers and good wishes coming and I'll be sure to pass along any messages anyone has.
> —Rita

Monday, March 26, 2007

> Hello again,
>
> Well the results came back and they weren't what we were hoping for. It's definitely cancer and five of 17 lymph nodes came back positive so that means chemo is definitely in our future. She'll have to heal from the surgery first so it may be a month or two before any treatment starts. So that's the bad news.
>
> The good news is she's off the IV and moved up to soft foods—pudding, cream soups, etc. She's moving around better and the pain has dropped off substantially. She took some pain meds this afternoon but declined to take any more this evening. It might have something to do with the fact that the pain meds on an almost empty stomach made her sick to her stomach so then she had to take something for that. Anyway, she continues to make strides in her recovery. Unfortunately, she's still on oxygen and she's not eating much and she's still very tired. The doctor said maybe she could go home tomorrow but he didn't say it in a very positive tone. I sensed he was leaning toward Wednesday.
>
> Visitors are always welcome but please keep the visits short. They do tire her out. I'll keep sending out updates and if anyone has any messages to pass along feel free to send them. Again, thank you to everyone for the cards and flowers, offers of assistance and all the good wishes. We really do have the greatest friends and family.
> —Rita

When I got stronger, I started writing the updates on CaringBridge. Since I'm a writer, this was a natural outlet for me to communicate my feelings and experiences. Here are two of the messages I wrote to my family and friends:

> *Friday, May 4, 2007*
> *It's a Beautiful Day!*
> *The port-catheter is in and I'm on my way to chemo . . . and how's your day going?*
>
> *I should really stop being so dramatic. I look over the week and find myself being silly. I was supremely anxious getting the staples out of my stomach when I had a port-catheter scheduled to be put in the next day. Hmmm, I think I need to seriously readjust my anxiety. I feel like the ultimate weenie. My apologies.*
>
> *The port-catheter is kind of a weird little device. It's a bit painful right now but that's because it's new and I'm not accustomed to it just yet. I give it five more minutes and I'll be fine. Now the nurses can take blood samples, inject chemo drugs, and put in contrast dyes for CT scans without having to put IV's in my hands and arms. Pretty darn groovy if you ask me.*
>
> *There've been so many changes lately, such as dropping twenty-five pounds. Since I've got the "most wonderful partner to share my life with," I think it best to concentrate on getting an appetite and gaining some weight back. The weight loss makes me feel and look fragile, but don't let this fool you. I'm still 100 percent feisty.*
>
> *Thanks to Freda for getting the lyrics to the song You Raise Me Up. I got goose bumps reading the lyrics. I still have to download the song to my iPod. Thanks to everyone who had comments about same-sex rights. In all of our hearts, I know*

we all want the same thing—to be in the hospital (or hospice) with our partners during times of trauma and crises.

The physical therapist and home health nurse are due to make visits today. It's my activity and stomach malfunction makeover. Gee, and to think I could be working and writing the copy for a new product or service. What was I thinking?

Have a super duper day. I don't know where I'm going but I'm on my way . . .

Love, Alex

Friday, May 11, 2007

It's 1:00 a.m. Friday Morning:

I prayed for sleep tonight. Guess you can see how my prayers are going. It's been a rough few hours. The side effects of chemo are showing up and I'm beyond hope of getting though the night without them. I just want to sleep to ease me from the pain and nausea. I knew the side effects would come—it was just a matter of time.

Gentle sleep where are you? Did I take one too many naps today? Oh that's right, I never slept once. I thought to myself, "Self, what will make you tired?" And I responded, "How about writing an update in the middle of the night." Naw, that's something a disturbed writer would do. I tried counting my blessings instead of sheep, but it didn't work. I tried writing out a prayer just so I could say I made an honest attempt, but the prayer is on the table and I'm wide awake.

We cried tonight—Rita and I. We cried because life right now isn't what we planned. We cried because the future is so unpredictable and we can't get our arms around it. We cried because we're scared, scared of what could happen and what might not happen. We cried for each other—because of the stress and strain we are under. I cried because my love *for Rita is so strong and eternal, and she cried because she loves me with every inch of her soul. Yes, I thank the Great Spirit for Rita, and all that she's done. She simply says her caring and deeds are how she copes. And I cried because of her words.*

In darkness I spill my guts. It's truth-time for the heart. I just wish I could sleep so I could forget for a bit that I've got cancer. I want to be working again and complaining about the gas prices and going to happy hours. I want to talk about future trips we're planning and how our summer schedule is packed with camping, Lynx games, and family get-togethers. Instead, there's a hollow sound that fills the days and weeks ahead. For the life of me, I can't change a darn thing. I can't even make myself sleepy—the woman who used to sleep for twelve hours at a time. How wicked cancer can be.

I'll go back and try again, and maybe, if my prayers and midnight writings converge, I'll sleep. If not, you may get another update in a few hours.

Sleep well, my friends.

Love, Alex

Some days were better than others and I tried to have a healthy attitude about cancer. I wasn't running away from reality. I didn't know if I'd survive. I didn't know if chemotherapy would work. I clung to life by a thin thread. I was so scared I would die, and yet, in the darkest moments of my cancer, I prayed for death. I had fought so many battles in my life—I didn't think I had the strength to battle again.

In the midst of all the chaos, Rita and I had a brave discussion about death. We voiced our fears and let the tears fall. We talked about updating our wills and our health care directives. We made an appointment to see an attorney so that, if I died, Rita would not have to worry about my last wishes. I wanted to make sure she would be financially sound, and I discussed with her the need to move forward and, hopefully, fall in love again.

In January 2010, my cancer came back. I had a second liver surgery to remove more cancer. During my recovery, however, I developed Acute Respiratory Distress Syndrome (ARDS). ARDS is a life-threatening lung condition that prevents enough oxygen from getting into the blood.

According to the National Institutes of Health, ARDS is caused by a major injury to the lung. Causes include breathing vomit into the lungs (aspiration), inhaling chemicals, pneumonia, and septic shock. ARDS "leads to a buildup of fluid in the air sacs. This fluid prevents enough oxygen from passing into the bloodstream. The fluid buildup also makes the lungs heavy and stiff, and decreases the lungs' ability to expand." Some symptoms of ARDS are severe breathing difficulties, low blood pressure, and organ failure. While around a third of people with ARDS die from the disease, survivors generally recover at least most of their lung function, although they often have some permanent lung damage. Survivors of ARDS can also have brain damage, which results from the brain not getting enough oxygen during the course of the disease.

Physicians and surgeons usually diagnose ARDS while treating another illness. For me the illness was cancer.

When I was diagnosed with ARDS, I wasn't even aware what was happening to me: I was in a medically induced coma. When I regained consciousness, I couldn't believe what cancer, two liver surgeries, and ARDS did to me. It became very clear that when the body goes through trauma (like surgery), it becomes more at risk for potentially chronic or life-threatening illnesses.

I can still remember the shock on the faces of Rita, friends, and family when I regained consciousness. I never want to see those frightened looks again.

After having four surgeries involving my abdomen, I developed hernias. (My surgeon told me the inside of my stomach looked like Swiss cheese.) I had to go through surgery again so a mesh could be placed inside to keep the hernias from bulging out. (I'm not making this stuff up—I know it seems like science fiction.) Once my hernia repair was healing, I was off to chemotherapy for the second time in three years.

Tools to Survive Cancer

Cancer isn't a one-person illness. When it occurs, cancer affects a community of people. Cancer changes our lives and makes us focus on the things that really matter. I've come to believe that we can survive cancer if we balance the connection of our mind, body, and spirit. To do that, I've discovered that I have the following tools to keep me alive.

1. Medication. Nobody likes to take pills or have injections, and certainly no one wants to have to go through chemotherapy or radiation treatment. Medication is a tool to help your body get what it doesn't have or doesn't have enough of. I went through two treatments of chemotherapy because it was one way (along with surgery) to get rid of the cancer cells in my body. Sure, I could have said no to chemo, and many people do, but I wanted to get rid of the cancer and increase my chances for living longer. I'm glad I had chemo. My oncologist did everything to minimize the side effects, but when you are infused with toxic drugs, you're going to have some nausea, fatigue, hair loss, etc. The one thing I can assure you, however, is that when the chemo stops, the side effects go away. Your hair grows back, and you have more energy. More importantly, medication like chemotherapy can keep your body alive.

You may have to convince yourself to go on a medication or to have chemo. It's a mind thing. If you can convince your mind and spirit, your body already knows it needs help. Taking a medication doesn't make you less of a human being. I take insulin, but that doesn't mean I'm weak or sick. Unfortunately, I saw myself as a sick child, and the more I thought that way, the worse I felt, and the harder it was to control my blood sugars. When I decided to take control of my daily diabetes routine, I no longer felt weak or sick. The same thing happened with cancer. At first I could hardly walk or function. I felt extremely fragile. But as time passed and I recovered from surgeries and chemo, I didn't feel I was sick. I tell my mind that I'm getting healthier, and my body responds by getting healthier. Don't let negative messages convince you not to go on a medication or not to have chemo or radiation. Getting treatment could save your life.

2. Neuromuscular therapy. While going through chemo the first time, I learned about a clinic that offered neuromuscular therapy (NT). I was intrigued and wondered if NT would help my side effects. I went into the clinic and asked a lot of questions about NT. To my surprise, I found NT to be the perfect antidote for chemo side effects (and for the other aches and pains I had).

According to the clinic I went to, called Benessere: Body in Balance, neuromuscular therapy "treats the cause of the pain rather than just the symptoms, resulting in lasting pain relief." It involves "a variety of soft tissue manipulation techniques, including trigger point release, static pressure (holding pressure for 8–12 seconds), passive movement of joints, and massage to improve circulation and relax muscles." Because of the cancer, my body went through the wringer. My muscles went into spasms, and my joints stiffened. Trying to sit at my desk and write became unbearable agony. When I found NT, I was pleased to see how my body responded. Tight muscles were relieved, toxic drugs that built up under the fascia were released, and my stomach and liver settled down.

I had many treatments. NT therapists are well-trained and knowledgeable about the body and how the body tries to hang on to stress and trauma. With gentleness, my NT therapist was able to give me full range of motion in both arms. I was surprised by the results. And I didn't need medication to subdue the pain. My NT therapist treated my pain at its source rather than treating the symptoms of the pain. NT isn't free and is not often covered by insurance, but it is a viable tool and an investment in your healing and well-being. I can't tell you how appreciative my body is for what NT has done.

3. Guided imagery. I was introduced to Belleruth Naparstek, a pioneer in guided imagery, or what she refers to as "applied imagination," when my therapist recommended I listen to Kanta Bosniak's audiobook *Surviving Cancer*. Listening to the CD opened my imagination and let my spirit soar. I was guided by imagery that made sense to me and made me feel powerful. I could take the cancer cells and, through imagery, destroy them. The affirmations at the end of the recording gave me new messages to say to myself rather than the life-defeating messages I had learned as a child. I felt in control over the cancer. My spirit was energized, my mind was calm but purposeful, and my body began to get stronger.

This is how Naparstek describes guided imagery in her book *Invisible Heroes*: "These imagery-based solutions use the right hemisphere of the brain—perception, sensation, emotion, and movement. . . . Trauma produces changes in the brain that impede a person's ability to think and talk about the event but that actually accentuate their capacity for imaging and emotional-sensory experiencing around it. Imagery uses what's most accessible in the traumatized brain to help with the healing."

4. Friends and relationships. This tool provides companionship and support. Positive people are mind and spirit candy. They give you a "zing" when you feel you're heading for a "splat"! Studies prove that talking honestly with a friend enhances not only your immune system but theirs as well. It's a win-win situation. Do you have to tell everything about how you're feeling to every friend? No. You can be

selective about whom you tell what to. Cultivate friends you can be serious with or friends who make you laugh yourself silly. No two friends are the same, but every friend is a gift.

Many research studies have found that our relationships influence our health and wellness. In the Renewing Life program, we often discuss three types of relationships. They are: draining (also known as toxic), nurturing, and nourishing. Toxic relationships make you feel drained, exhausted, anxious, and smothered. Your relationships with toxic people can actually make you sick. If you feel these relationships are otherwise worthy, you will need to constantly work on them.

The next type of relationship is nurturing (also known as neutral). These relationships are important to your survival. These are people who can hear you talk about your illness, but if you start talking about your emotions and feelings, they will probably not engage with you. They will say things such as "You'll be fine," or "Let's not talk about this anymore." These are people in your life who send you cards, bring flowers, cook meals, and bake cookies. They are important, but they are not able to delve into your heart issues (or their own).

The third relationship is called "nourishing." Nourishing relationships inspire you, are authentic, and model healthy behaviors. These relationships are energy-creating and vital to your healing. Also, these relationships support you physically and emotionally and give you hope.

5. Gratitude. Speaking of being grateful, gratitude is a "must use" tool. I've sent hundreds of handwritten thank-you notes to all the people who helped me in my fight with cancer. I've also said a million thank-you prayers to the Great Spirit. From the bottom of my soul, I want to thank everyone for being there for me. I am constantly grateful to live another day. I constantly thank Rita for keeping me alive. I constantly thank the prayer chain that went from

Minnesota to Wisconsin, to New Jersey, to Poland, to New Zealand, to Hawaii, to California, to Nebraska, and back to Minnesota. I'm sure the angels in heaven worked overtime to register all the prayers on my account. As I've said so often, I could not have survived without the thousands of prayers I received—a lot of them from people I didn't even know.

Cancer made me humble and grateful. Not that I wasn't humble and grateful before, but now I know how important it is to feel grateful. Now, gratitude is a part of every moment in my life.

How deep does my gratitude run? I surprised myself after a year of living with cancer when I said to Rita, "You know, I'm grateful for having cancer." She gave me a puzzled look. I told her, "If it hadn't been for the diagnosis, I probably would have had a very short life. The cancer diagnosis and treatment extended my life. The fact is, if it hadn't been for the cancer diagnosis and the treatment, I would not be alive today. I think that's something to be grateful for."

Here are two CaringBridge entries that exemplify my endless gratitude:

Tuesday, December 18, 2007
  Happy Holidays:
  I'm sitting here with my dog on my lap and feeling a rush of emotion. (I'm calling this multi-tasking as I give Bob a massage. He's watching me type and sighing. I guess everyone's an editor.) I spent two and a half hours wrapping gifts today and thinking of all the people who kept me alive this Christmas. I have to tell you, this is the most meaningful Christmas of my life. I've often said that if you could apply a dollar amount to friendship, I would be the wealthiest woman in the world. I've been given the gifts of friends, family and life. How could I not be sentimental this Christmas?

I went to see my oncologist today for a check-up. My white blood count continues to be low, so once again I'm being cautioned about being around sick people this holiday season. I'm fighting a cold and so everyone is on hyper-alert. But I'm forcing the fluids and taking good care of myself. Not to worry.

I stood in line at the post office yesterday to buy two stamps. It only took an hour. I looked around me and saw so many people in ugly moods. I bet they didn't have a life-crisis this year to make them grateful for standing in a line. I wanted to jump on the counter and tell them that life is good, despite the wars. But joy comes in minutes not months. I was smiling and I know people thought I was insane.

This Saturday we'll be traveling to Rochester to spend Christmas with Rita's family. Then Sunday morning we're off to Wisconsin again for my family's Christmas. I'm looking forward to this trip because I haven't seen some of my relatives since my cancer diagnosis. I pray I don't end up in the hospital again like in October. (My oncologist thinks I had a major chemo drug reaction and that's why I ended up in the hospital.)

Bob just farted and I have to go outside and get some fresh air. I hope your day is going well and nobody's farting where you are.

Love, Alex

Friday, December 21, 2007
Season's Greetings:
As Christmas approaches and the New Year is just a hint away, I wanted to take this moment to stop and be sentimental. (No, not againnnnnnn!)
Yes, sentimental me.
I want to thank each one of you for following my journey

through cancer this year. It was a frightening year but my spirit was lifted again and again by your guestbook entries, emails, cards, phone calls and visits. Your presence in my life gave me the courage to hang on even when the odds were so stacked against me. Your kind words and generosity were medicine to my soul. I'm humbled by your support.

My deepest thanks for the bunny slippers, bracelets and necklaces, colon cancer angel pin, flowers and plants, meals and more meals, groceries, games and books, meditation tapes and massages, music, cards and letters, stuffed animals, pajamas, DVD's, yappy hours, the loaning of mom's wedding ring and angel pin, donations to CaringBridge, donations to the Relay for Life event, crocheted hats, house cleaning, haircuts, computer repairs, hugs and kisses, hand holding, haircuts, walks, visits, emails, phone calls, prayers and more prayers, physical support when I could barely walk, friendship, and love.

I'm blessed by your gifts and that you kept me in your thoughts throughout the year. "You raise me up" with your never-ending support and encouragement. You comforted Rita while she faced painful decisions and an unpredictable future. My gratitude to her is immeasurable.

This Christmas I was given the gift of life. I got all the trimmings, too—friendship, love, commitment, and support. From the bottom of my heart and soul, thank you for keeping me going. I needed you and you were there. Thank you.

Have a merry Christmas and a joyous new year.

Love, Alex

Before you fall asleep tonight, send out at least one thank-you to someone (here or in heaven) who helped you today—it strengthens your immune system.

ACTIVITY 12

Reflect on Your Friendships

NEVER GIVE UP

SUPPLIES: pen or pencil and paper, or a computer

How do we develop friendships? Is it shared interests? Shared values? Shared joy? Did we come together because we shared our problems? Is it a little of all or some of these things?

What do you really value in a friendship?

Think of a close friend. What do you value in this person? Is your relationship energy-enhancing or energy-draining?

- What do you love and respect about this person? List some of these qualities.
- Now list some of your friend's weaknesses.
- List the strengths and weaknesses that you bring to the friendship.

Reflect on these questions on your own or with a friend:

- Do you and your friend share strengths and weaknesses?
- How are you different from one another?
- Overall, are you uplifted and enhanced by the relationship?
- Do you feel joy when you're together?

Never Give Up

4

Living with Your New Changes

Your New Normal

"When are you going to get back to your old self again?"
"I'm looking forward to seeing the old Alex."
"I miss the old Alex."
"After chemo, won't it be great to get back to normal life again?"

Normal life? I was diagnosed with stage 4 cancer and a life-threatening illness, and I'd survived two near-death experiences. Who can be "normal" after that?

While recovering from four surgeries and chemotherapy, I frequently heard these kinds of questions and comments. But I knew in my soul that I had been profoundly changed. Could I return to the "old" Alex? I'd gained too much wisdom and insight to go back to being her.

My "new" normal takes friends and family by surprise. This fascinates me because I know I'm not the same person I was before I had cancer. I'm not afraid of things the way I used to be. I also don't worry unless someone (like my oncologist) tells me I should worry. Living with cancer gives me a confidence I didn't have. I know now that I can survive whatever life throws at me.

A serious or life-threatening illness is not an inconvenience—something to get over. It's always life-altering and a time for personal transformation. Cancer made me reevaluate my priorities and values. Physically, emotionally, and spiritually, I stopped taking life for granted.

My initial, physical response to trauma is always to FIGHT. But I've found out the hard way what happens when I don't maintain a healing mind-body-spirit balance. Fighting cancer cells is tough. My body did what it could do. Then as I dealt with sleep apnea and cancer, I found that during sleep our bodies heal. I find this amazing. I have the tools within me to keep my body healthy. If I gain weight, I know how to take it off safely. If I party too much with friends, I know the next day I will need time to rest. If my back aches after cleaning the house, I know I need to stretch my muscles to ease the strain. Taking care of our physical bodies doesn't have to be complex. I've started to make an effort to simply stand in front of the mirror every day and say, "I love my body."

My initial *emotional* response to trauma is always to FLEE. I know that taking care of my feelings is a bit more difficult. It was easy for me to stuff my feelings so I didn't have to face them. Fleeing was a learned response when I knew I couldn't express my feelings. Now, facing them on a daily basis is both a direct and an authentic approach. If I deal with the sadness or anger of today, I won't have to be bothered by them tomorrow. It sure makes sleeping much more peaceful.

My initial *spiritual* response to trauma is always to FREEZE. This is like a deer getting caught in your headlights. It's natural for them to freeze. Many of us are like that.

I didn't flee from cancer; instead I practiced being authentic. Becoming authentic means being the real person you are meant to be. You clear away all the old beliefs and actions that no longer work for you. By being authentic, I align my emotions with my heart and my actions with my energy. I dump the "shoulds" and clear out the old ways that harmed me in the past.

I love this quote from two cancer therapists, Carl and Stephanie Simonton, mentioned in the Renewing Life program:

> You must stop and reassess your priorities and values. You must be willing to be yourself, not what people want you to be because you think that this is the only way you can get love. You can no longer be dishonest. You are now at a point where, if you truly want to live, you have to be who you are.

I've come to understand that if I truly want to live I have to be who I am.

Tools for Coping with Your New Normal

These tools can help you adjust to your new normal.

1. Make friends with your body parts. Your trauma, loss, or illness may have left you with physical scars, aches, and pains. I learned through guided imagery to make friends with my body parts. It wasn't easy. I first had to hear what my physical body had to say. My body was angry with me for not accepting the changes it went through, especially since it tried so hard to keep me alive. I looked in the mirror and began to talk directly to my physical body. I told it that I was grateful for the healing it had done. My scars were not ugly, as I had claimed, but were now medals of honor. Then I thanked my body parts for staying with me and keeping me alive. Finally, my body parts thanked me for hearing what they had to say. I go back and talk to them frequently, so I know how my body parts are feeling. This really works. Try it.

2. Accept your limitations. Since my stomach endured multiple surgeries, I can't wear clothes that are tight around my waist. Tight waistbands may be the style, but for this body I no longer wear them.

I also lost my ability to balance on one leg. It seems my center has shifted, and I continue to fall to the right. I have to be very careful when I'm putting on my pants. I frequently crash against the dresser to catch my balance. The mesh screen that was surgically installed to keep my hernias from popping out keeps causing pain. I can't just jump into bed anymore. I have to sit down first, bring my knees up, and gently lean back into the mattress. When I walk a lot, I need to take breaks to sit down and rest my legs and feet. Some would call this a sign of aging, but I'm not ready to go there yet.

3. Test your memory. With taking so many drugs during my cancer, including chemotherapy, I now forget things. (Again, some may say this is a normal sign of aging.) I seem to have kept my long-term memory in place, but I have some short-term memory loss. I find I've got word search problems. As a writer I'm devastated. By the time I reach the end of a chapter I'm reading or even writing, I can't remember what was going on in the beginning. I work on these memory issues by using games to keep my mind challenged. If you can't recall things, just allow your mind to search through millions of stored memories. Don't get frustrated—this happens to all of us. If your memory loss is severe, see a memory specialist or a physician for help.

4. Try new challenges. For those of us who are prone to frequent feelings of anxiousness, we often avoid new experiences and challenges, but that's the last thing we should do. Trying new experiences actually widens our comfort zone and increases our ability to survive. Our lives are constantly changing—whether we like it or not. New jobs, new relationships, and new beginnings require us to adapt faster to new technology and communications than in the past. If you don't adapt to these changes, you may experience a feeling of loss and loneliness.

New experiences also have positive emotional effects. We learn new skills, increase our knowledge, and develop a feeling of confidence. If we fail at first, we learn that we may have to finesse our thinking or modify our behavior. Challenges happen daily, but the good news is that we learn from every experience we face. Taking risks can increase your self-confidence and self-esteem. The more we try new challenges, the more support we gain from family, friends, and coworkers.

5. Live in the moment. The past is in the past, the future is in the future, and the present is here and now. There are many ugly things in life. First of all, acknowledge your past, and be grateful for the incidents that propelled you forward. You don't have to live there anymore. What a relief. The same goes for incidents in your future. Why worry and get yourself sick? All we have is the precious present. In this moment you can choose to be sad or joyful. Visit nature and marvel over the beauty and tranquility. Do you want to interrupt this moment with anger or fear?

It's so easy to give up and walk away from transforming our life into something healthier and happier. If you chose to make changes, remember to never give up.

ACTIVITY 13

Reflect on Your New Normal

NEVER GIVE UP

SUPPLIES: pen or pencils

How do you think about your life after experiencing a major event or crisis? Some cancer survivors refer to their diagnosis as a "wake-up call." No matter what you call the event, you know you've been changed—sometimes physically but more often emotionally. You're dealing with a new normal.

The loss of a job or the diagnosis of an illness can make you feel as if you were dropped on your head. When you get back up, you don't feel like yourself.

In the chart below, list events that contributed to your new normal. You may want to discuss these changes with family and friends.

EVENT	WHAT WERE YOU LIKE BEFORE THE EVENT	WHAT ARE YOU LIKE AFTER THE EVENT?
September 11, 2001	Before, I felt safe and secure.	Now, I am more cautious.

Setbacks in Healing

In the Middle of Between

In the middle of between there's no room
for indecision; only room enough
to be alone, in the center of the road.
I can see the light at both ends, but which
end do I travel, which way is the right one;
in the middle of between.

From one end to the other, to and fro and back
again at the midpoint, where do I stand on
any given point in the midst of knowing
too little; unable to reach the peak.
Never empty, never full, there is no mean,
In the middle of between.

—Alex Acker-Halbur

Setbacks. Every trauma and every illness includes setbacks. It's almost as if the Great Spirit wants to remind us of where we've been and how far we've come. I know that there's a reason why setbacks exist.

In January 2008, following the year I was diagnosed with cancer, I held a chemo- and cancer-free party. All my friends and family came to help me celebrate being cancer-free. I had had my last chemo session two weeks earlier, and I was scheduled to have a PET scan the Monday after the party, but I just knew the scan would find nothing. So I celebrated my new health, and everything that night was perfect.

The PET scan found something. My oncologist couldn't tell if it was an active cancer lesion or possibly scar tissue on my liver, so he had me in for a follow-up MRI. The MRI found cancer.

I was devastated and embarrassed. I had eighty of my favorite friends and family to my house to celebrate that I was cancer-free, but I wasn't. The impression that I gave them was false hope. I wanted to crawl into a hole and never come out.

Instead of more chemo, I was scheduled for several CyberKnife procedures. According to PeaceHealth Southwest Medical Center in Vancouver, Washington:

> Stereotactic radiosurgery is a non-invasive (non-surgical) treatment in which high doses of focused radiation beams are delivered from multiple locations outside the body to destroy a tumor or lesion within the body. This procedure does not remove the tumor or lesion. Instead, it destroys tumor cells or stops the growth of active tissue. . . . Using x-ray image cameras and computer technology similar to that used for cruise missile guidance, the CyberKnife locates the tumor in the body. A computer program has an arsenal of over 1200 beam angles to choose from to cover the tumor and spare normal tissues.

Just imagine a guided missile that destroys cancer cells. No blood and pain involved. Doesn't this sound like something out of a science fiction movie?

For me, this was a setback. It was the middle of between. My mind and spirit were ready to move on, but my body dug in its heels and said, "Hey, hold on a second." I was depressed.

When I took time to think about it, I realized I had overreacted. Once I did my homework and found out what was involved with the CyberKnife procedure, I felt a bit foolish for whining that I had to have another surgery. The CyberKnife is not a surgery but a medical procedure, one that's been around for thirty years. I was comforted by knowing that there were no side effects like with chemo, and that I wouldn't have to be cut open again.

Yes, I did overreact to the cancer. How could I not? The word "cancer" itself ignites fear, and an active cancer lesion fuels terror. I had to stop myself from going downhill fast. I had to look at the cancer with a different perspective. Rather than having cancer in my colon, lymph nodes, and liver, I had one spot on my liver that needed to be addressed—one spot versus many. From this perspective I could take a deep breath and let it out slowly. I could deal with one spot, one more time.

Some setbacks are worse than others, but I've come to realize that if you believe the setback is going to be terrible, it will be. That's why it's important to put the setback into proper perspective. For me trauma and illness setbacks are the most personal. In many situations, the setback may be a life-or-death situation. (Although financial, career, and relationship setbacks may feel like a life-or-death situation at the time, they rarely are.) Trauma and illness setbacks hit emotionally hard, probably because of the belief "if you don't have your health, you have nothing."

I was unemployed at the time of my cancer diagnosis. If I hadn't had Rita to rely on, I would have lost my home and health insurance and would have become reliant on state services. In my research, I found that people who have no insurance and are diagnosed with cancer have a higher death rate than people who have insurance.

With the current cost of health care, it's a "crisis" in all directions.

When setbacks occur, do you fall apart or bounce back? The ability to bounce back is also known as resilience. Many studies prove that people with resilience have inner strengths and are able to snap back more quickly from setbacks.

People who aren't resilient often feel like victims, are easily overwhelmed, and may resort to unhealthy coping mechanisms, such as chemical abuse. They are also at risk of developing physical and emotional problems.

Change and trauma have become the new normal in today's world. Resilience strengthens your immune system so that your mind-body-spirit can fight against anxiety, depression, and post-traumatic stress disorder (PTSD). In Chapter 1 I discussed the effects of stress. This is one area where resilience can save your mental and physical well-being.

Being resilient doesn't mean that setbacks won't happen. What resilience can do is help you cope with your challenges. When you identify and develop resilience skills, you'll be able to handle setbacks.

After all the CyberKnife appointments and x-rays, it was determined the cancer in my liver was too complex and difficult for the CyberKnife procedure. Instead, I went through liver surgery for a second time to remove the cancer lesion.

Tools for Coping with Setbacks

Becoming resilient in order to handle setbacks is an individual experience. Adapt the following tools for your own situation, keeping in mind what has or has not worked for you in the past. Here are some resiliency tools you can use today.

1. Get connected. Setbacks can often make us feel isolated. This is an important time to connect with friends and nature. Pets are also great because they listen without judgment.

2. Live in the moment. Take several deep breaths to relax your body and mind. Place your concerns outside while you breathe. Trust me, your concerns will be happy to annoy you again. As you practice deep breathing, remember you're also strengthening your resilience.

3. Have hope. Setbacks often trigger our fears. If you can, replace those fears with hope. Read poetry or books on developing hope.

4. Anticipate change. Fear is often the first response to change. Luckily, you already know how you've handled past setbacks. You know what works and what doesn't. Use this knowledge to expand your ways of accepting change. Anticipating change takes away the fear of setbacks.

5. Acknowledge your setbacks. Your setbacks won't go away. If you can find a meaning for the setback, you'll be able to bounce back more quickly. Fear needs silence to grow. When you mentally and physically acknowledge a setback, you remove the fear.

6. Find a benefit. We all have setbacks; there are no exceptions. Try to find some good out of the setback, even though it may be small. Identifying something good that came out of a setback lessens the pain or grief.

7. Use humor and laughter. Appropriate expressions of humor and laughter during setbacks are healing. We laugh to lighten our hearts. If you can't find humor in your situation, try watching funny movies or going to comedy clubs. Identify the people in your life who make you laugh.

8. Think better of yourself. Setbacks can cause your self-esteem and self-confidence to plummet. Take time to nurture your self-image

and be proud of yourself. Stand in front of a mirror, and tell yourself how strong and courageous you are. Why? Because you are!

9. Maintain perspective. Don't belittle yourself or compare yourself with others who are experiencing a similar situation. This can increase your depression and hamper your healing. You're an important person in our universe. Know that you can manage your setback if you work at it.

If you don't feel you're making the kind of progress you'd like, or you just don't know where to start, consider talking to a mental health professional about developing resilience. You don't have to have a diagnosed mental disorder to talk to a therapist. With their guidance, you can be positive and attain emotional well-being.

Remember that setbacks don't have to delay your healing. With the right tools you can overcome them. Coping with setbacks takes time and patience, but you can learn how to act or control how you respond to a setback.

ACTIVITY 14

Cope with Setbacks

SUPPLIES: pens or colored pencils or pastels

Holding onto a setback keeps you stuck. Some people become depressed when they encounter a setback, while others find effective ways to move on. Did you know that our brains are wired to pay more attention to negative experiences? It's a self-protective characteristic from many, many generations ago, when we faced predators in the wild.

Start to rewire your brain with clear messages on how to cope with setbacks. Write phrases next to and around the image of the brain. For best results, repeat these messages three or four times a day until they are embedded in your mind.

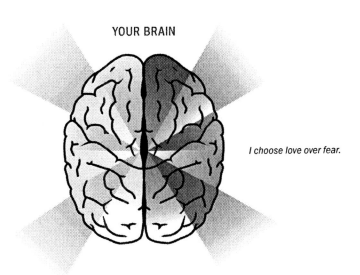

YOUR BRAIN

I choose love over fear.

NEVER GIVE UP

5

Understanding Death— Yours and Your Loved Ones'

Death as a New Beginning

Very few people want to talk about their deaths. I know I didn't want to. Cancer, however, made me face my death. Though I found death to be a difficult topic, talking about it with my loved ones was a moving experience.

Before my cancer diagnosis, I thought death was the final trauma. Death was something I feared. I watched my mom struggle for nine months before she died. She was in constant pain, and she didn't want to die. Her experience frightened me. I wondered, *Is there life after death? Is death final? Where do we go when we die? What does it feel like? Will I be able to join my deceased loved ones?*

After two near-death experiences, I'm convinced that there is life after death. Death is not final. I hold the knowledge that my energy will be released into the universe and I'll find the peace, joy, and happiness I've always wanted. I'm no longer afraid to die because it's really a beginning.

At other times in my life I have wanted to die. I've come to realize that this was my way of saying, "I'm terrified, and I want the abuse and the pain to end." I admit that I thought about suicide a lot.

Death is a reality. And a beginning.

Right after I had colon surgery, I woke up in the middle of the night in a lot of pain. I was still in shock from the cancer diagnosis, and I prayed that the cancer would take me quickly. It was the blackest moment for me, and I knew my body, mind, and spirit were all hovering between life and death. My body hurt, my mind was stunned, and my spirit was depleted. I could hardly move. Seconds ticked by very slowly as I waited on the threshold. I couldn't see any hope for the future, and my past was, well, in the past. I shivered and felt all the warmth leave my body. I was so cold.

Something similar happened after I had my second liver surgery. The cancer had metastasized into my liver, and I had to have a spot removed. The surgery was a nightmare. While the surgeon was in my abdomen, he removed my gallbladder, too. (I didn't even know I had gallstones.) During the night I awoke from a dark dream. My body again was filled with pain, and I called the nurse for more medication. The nurse came in and told me I couldn't have more medication. I started to cry. She told me she would talk with the doctor on call to see what they could do for me. As the door shut, I lay in the dark, feeling myself hanging in a tenuous state. I could feel my body dropping into the mattress, deeper and deeper. I couldn't make the motion stop.

I started thinking about the talk Rita and I had about death. It wasn't the greatest conversation I've ever had with her, but one we had to have. She told me then she would keep going but would probably not get into another relationship. I was shocked. I looked at her very closely. She was still beautiful and had energy to reach her dreams. She wanted to travel but wanted me to be a part of her travels. I wanted to be a part of them, too. We kept talking and crying. I told her that love would find her again. I saw the lines of exhaustion on her face and the fear in her eyes. Those green eyes glistening with tears: they pleaded with me not to leave her.

How could I leave her? She'd given up three whole years of her life to be by my side during the cancer surgeries and treatment. Every moment she thought of my needs, putting her own on hold. She was there in my hospital room every morning and was the last one to leave at night. She wiped my tears when I cried and read me funny emails to make me laugh. Rita lined up people to be with me when she had meetings at work. She made sure I was comfortable, and she talked to the nurses and doctors when I was in pain. Rita made decisions for me that I couldn't make myself, asked questions, and did research. Luckily, for both of us, the hospital staff was very aware and accommodating of our relationship and never asked Rita to leave. She became one of the nurses, finding me more blankets, pillows, and ice chips.

How could I leave her that night?

That night, after all the years of pain, abuse, and illness, I realized I wasn't ready to die.

The nurse came back in and gave me some more pain medication. I slept for more hours that night than I had during the course of my cancer. It was a restful, refueling sleep. The pain was drifting away, and my spirit seemed to be lifting. I could make it. I would make it.

We all know that death is inevitable. After that night I no longer fear death the way I did during the initial phases of cancer. I'd made peace with myself. I'd do everything I could to get healthier. I'd write the book that I said I'd write after my throat surgery. I'd fulfill the promises I made to myself and others. I would not waste all the prayers that were made on my behalf. I'd move on from the abuse and the cancer to live a meaningful life. I'd take all of my tools and polish and strengthen them. I'd start believing in my goals and in myself, and I'd reach out to the Great Spirit for guidance and direction. I'd listen carefully and act on my inspiration and passion.

I also don't fear death because I believe in an afterlife. It doesn't matter to me if I come back as another human being or as a precious pinecone. I know I'll have a purpose—a meaning for my existence. I can come back as a bright star in the night sky or a supernova sending out waves of light and rays of energy into the universe. The energy I release will be positive, nurturing, and healing.

This is why I believe so strongly in my message, "Never Give Up." We can't give up because our spirit and energy float into the universe when we cease to breathe.

Upon reviewing this book, my dear friend Paul Berry, a psychologist, asked me, "Are we not meant to seek the wisdom of truth, love, and peace to share with others, whatever the cost, and carry it forward with us to another phase of the life cycle, ever searching more for wholeness?" My simple reply is yes. Yes, the energy we put out into the universe will never cease.

What will you be doing in your new beginning?

Tools to Face Death

Facing death is never easy, but these tools helped me feel up to the challenge.

1. Preparation. The first thing Rita and I did was to write our wills and create new health care directives. Now that we had experience with the health care system, we knew what we wanted and what we didn't. We spoke to an attorney several times about our wills, and months later we were relieved to have these documents completed and certified by a notary public. (You can find forms online to prepare your own will, but you may benefit from consulting an experienced estate planning attorney.)

2. Passion. There are certain things I do because I'm passionate about them. Writing fiction is pure rapture for me, and I'm passionate about character development (even the evil villain), settings, and

story lines. Passion is a motivator for me. Don't be fooled that you only find passion during sex. You can find passion in sunrises and sunsets. A garden. An old car. Colors. Music. Dance. Passion makes you feel alive. The passion to live is one of the best tools in your tool kit. You may have to find "things or people" to help strengthen your desire to stay alive.

3. Positive images. One night in the hospital I told Rita that I wanted to return to Italy with her and eat at a vineyard, drink wine, and watch the sunset. She told me to hold on to that image, and I did. We made the trip three years later.

4. Strength. During cancer, I realized that to become stronger I had to change my thoughts. It's as simple and uncomplicated as that. Start saying something different to yourself during tough times. When you feel stress, coach yourself, "You are strong. You can take this on. You are brave and resilient." (More on strength in Chapter 19.)

5. Gratitude. Several times a day I'll stop myself and tell the Great Spirit how grateful I am for all the things I've been given. Times like when I'm driving down the road and I see a rainbow in the sky, or four white-tailed deer running through my backyard at dusk. Here's a sample you can use to state your gratitude: "Dear [the one you pray to], thank you for [specific event] because it reminds me I'm alive and loved."

6. Hope. Hope is eternal. If we have something to hope for (like staying alive), our body, mind, and spirit get together to make it so. Studies show that having a sense of hope strengthens our immune system.

ACTIVITY 15

Choose 10 Meaningful Things to Do Before You Die

SUPPLIES: pen and paper or audio recorder

Some people don't even get the chance to do one meaningful thing before they die. Work on this activity while you still have your health and physical and emotional skills. You may want people around you, or you might like to think about these things when you are alone.

1. Have meaningful conversations with the special people in your life. Tell them how much you love them.
2. If you fear pain, ask your medical or hospice staff for ways they can make your passing more comfortable.
3. If you have a grudge against a family member or friend, talk directly to that person and make an effort to resolve the problem.
4. Get rid of your regrets.
5. Share your stories. Have a relative or friend bring in photos of you, so you can talk about what you were doing and feeling at the time the picture was taken.
6. Hold hands with loved ones.
7. Pray.
8. Ask for all your friends and family to be with you when you take your last breath.
9. Listen to your favorite songs.
10. Feel at one with the universe, and know your life is great.

Nothing in life is to be feared. It is only to be understood. Now is the time to understand more, so that we may fear less.

—Marie Curie, physicist and chemist

Death by Suicide

Why do people commit suicide? I'm not an expert, but I can tell you why adults abused as children or women who've been raped or sexually exploited do. It's because of an extreme sense of loss, the loss of childhood; the loss of self, self-esteem, and self-image; the loss of self-confidence and self-identity; the loss of trust, faith, and relationships; the loss of safety, physical wellness, emotional health; the loss of hope; and the loss of dreams. All of this can be what drives people to commit suicide.

Loss

Every time my father sexually assaulted me, I took the rage I had for him and I turned it inside. When I was raped, I took the rage for my rapist and turned it inside. When my college therapist sexually exploited me, I took the rage for her and turned it inside. I hated myself. All that rage boiled inside me, and I couldn't find a way to let it go. I couldn't live in this much pain. I had to end it.

Instead I found a technique to handle my rage: self-talk. Here's an example of my self-talk when I was considering suicide:

MY INNER VOICE: Hey Alex!
ME: Yeah, what do you want?
INNER VOICE: I noticed that you're thinking about suicide again.
ME: I have so much rage about all the abuse. I just want it all to end.
INNER VOICE: And you think suicide is the answer.
ME: I'm at the end of my rope. I can't take much more of this pain.
INNER VOICE: You know you're strong and brave, right?
ME: I don't feel that way right now.
INNER VOICE: You also know that you didn't cause the abuse, rape, and sexual exploitation. You aren't responsible for these things—you're only responsible for getting help.
ME: You mean like seeing my therapist about this rage.
INNER VOICE: Exactly. Deep in your heart I know you don't want to die. Am I right about this?
ME: Well yes, but I'm so scared.
INNER VOICE: We both are. How about if we call 911?
ME: Well, yeah, I think I can do this.
INNER VOICE: I know you can, and I support you.

Physical and emotional pain can drive us to suicide, but we can stop the pain and get help.

If you're considering suicide, I'm asking you to get help immediately. Call a friend you trust, a crisis or suicide hotline, or 911. These are your tools to help you never give up.

In every one of us, we have tools that got us this far. Maybe the tools you've been using have become ineffective—like using a hammer rather than a saw to cut up a log. I see a therapist to help me in my dark moments. I can spill my guts and vomit the rage. My therapist knows what to do with it. She is trained to help me get it all out. When I decide to get all that puke and anger out of me, I can begin to get healthy. Many times I have held my rage inside. I didn't talk about the abuse because it was so dark. Then I'd get sick—really sick. I developed migraines, diabetes, high blood pressure, kidney disease, osteoarthritis, and even cancer. If I had puked my rage out years ago, I believe I would have had fewer physical illnesses and diseases in my life.

One of the most useful tools I use is therapy. At first I hated the thought of telling someone about all the abuse and the pain—having to live that agony all over again. But I knew deep inside that if I didn't go to therapy I was as good as gone. If I didn't actively end my life, all I had to do was wait for my body to get sick and die.

Looking back, I know my thoughts of suicide were calls for help—a need to have someone help me understand my memories and pain. I needed someone to help me learn to live again.

I believe that my unexpressed rage turned into cancer, so when two feet of my colon and parts of my liver were removed, I celebrated.

Okay. I didn't celebrate at first. Over time, when I was able to put the pieces of my life together—my new normal—I knew in my soul that the abuse had been cut out and removed. Then I did a happy dance.

Tools to Prevent Suicide

Guns, knives, ropes, and pills are not tools. They are weapons of self-destruction. If you're going to reach for one of these, STOP. You have better tools within you to get through loss and trauma.

1. Self-talk. Use positive self-talk to boost your self-confidence and self-esteem.

2. Emergency help. Call a crisis or suicide hotline when you have thoughts about harming yourself.

3. Professional help. Contact a therapist. If you don't have one, ask the crisis or suicide hotline for a recommendation.

Stop before you act. Don't pick up a gun. Pick up the phone. Please.

Never.
Never.
Never.

Never. Give. Up.

ACTIVITY 16

Create Your Success Chart

SUPPLIES: pens or pencils, paper

You are successful. You are a good person. As Stuart Smalley says (Al Franken's character on *Saturday Night Live*), "I'm good enough. I'm smart enough. And doggone it, people like me."

Sometimes you look back on your life and see only your failures and mistakes. You may compare yourself to supermodels, superheroes, professional athletes, celebrities, and wealthy people. Society has taught us that *they* are successful. We forget how successful we really are. We got this far—we must have done something right. Right?

Rather than focus on your mistakes—because everyone makes mistakes—let's focus on what you've done right. No matter how small, focus on what you've done well. Focus on smiles, laughter, joy, and goodness. Focus on kindness. Focus on giving—giving to yourself! Do this exercise with the focus on yourself. Reward yourself. Remember, *you* are good enough, you are smart enough, and doggone it, people like you!

"Success" is defined as anything that makes you feel good, happy, and excited. It can be as simple as a smile directed at someone you don't know. It can be an award you received. It could be homemade soup you sent to someone.

For each year of your life list a success. Here are a few examples:

1	2	3	4	5	6	7	8	9	10
	Learned how to walk	Learned to talk in sentences		Went to school for the first time		Rode my first bike		Aced my spelling test	Got my first puppy

31	32	33	34	35	36	37	38	39	40
Got my first apartment	Received my Master's Degree		Met the man/woman of my dreams		Got married		Purchased our first house		Went back to work

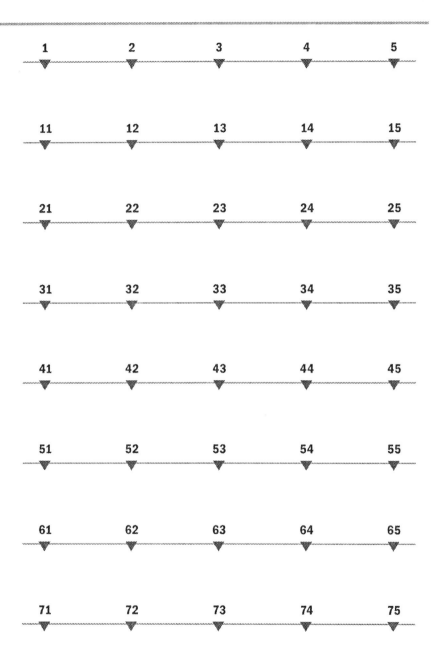

Now it's your turn. See how successful you are?

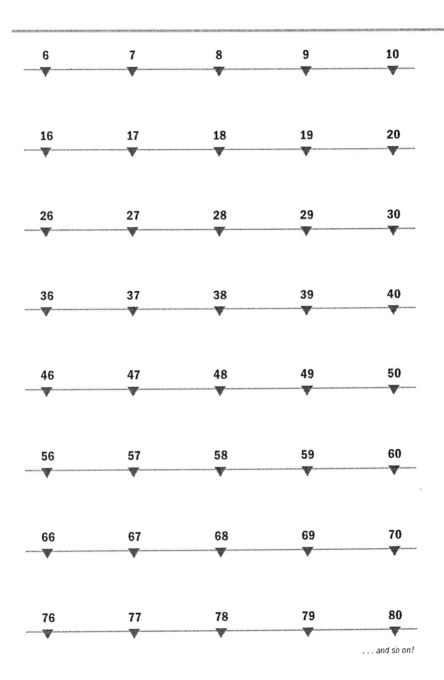

... and so on!

Look at this chart often, and remember the people who love you!

How to Talk with Your Dying Loved Ones

What the dying person needs is someone
to hear who they are and what their life is and has been.
—**Lawrence LeShan**

Losing a loved one is traumatic and fear-inducing. This fear, in turn, reduces our quality of life and takes precious moments away from those we deeply love. Many books address this fear, such as Dr. Lawrence LeShan's *Cancer as a Turning Point: A Handbook for People with Cancer, Their Families, and Health Professionals*. I also encourage you to use the tools at the end of this chapter throughout the grieving process.

What kind of statements and questions are useful in helping our loved ones move peacefully to their deaths? I give you some examples below, but don't read them verbatim to your loved one. Use your own words to ask questions that reflect your interest in their answers. Remember, you are not a therapist—you are a friend or family member who wants to hear the wisdom of your loved one's life. Trust your authentic self, being true to yourself while being gentle to others, to know when it's the right time to discuss certain questions. The best gift you can give to your dying loved one is to listen to their answers.

What if your loved one appears to be unconscious or unresponsive, or is deaf? Research indicates that the sense of hearing is the last to go. The brain, in fact, functions six to ten minutes after the heart stops. There are, however, many forms of communication other than talking. Touch can relay as much as, if not more than, words. Remember your hands reinforce your words, and vice versa. Gentle, loving thoughts that are vocalized will be affirmed by your touching.

- What's the best thing that ever happened to you? What's the worst? Why?
- What are the biggest achievements you've made in your life? What did these achievements mean to you?
- Are there any goals you wanted to achieve or adventures you wanted to have but didn't? Why?
- What was the best period of your life? What was the worst?
- If you were asked by a child to tell them the one most important thing that you have learned or done, what would you say?
- If you could change one decision in your life, what would it be?
- Do you see a theme to your life? If so, what is it?
- For the things that others did to you, what do you need to do in order to forgive them? For the things that happened to you, what do you need to forgive yourself?
- What do you need to finish your life, to complete it? Can you do it now?
- What do you feel is the longest part of the day for you? What do you mostly feel and think during this time?

- If you were to overhear your friends talking about you at your end-of-life celebration, what would you most like to hear them say about you? What would you least like to hear?

These are also excellent questions to ask yourself. They may motivate you to reach your goals.

Know the Truth

Here are some truths about death and ways you can help yourself through this special journey.

- No matter how long you've prepared for your loved one's death, when someone we're emotionally involved with dies, we're not prepared. It is always a shock if we have been emotionally connected to the person.
- Expect yourself to react at the time of your loved one's death. Responses of crying, sobbing, anger, disbelief, denial, and numbness are all natural. Allow your mind, body, and spirit time to adjust to this deep loss.
- Ask your loved ones the above questions to help you learn about his/her life. This helps both of you and leaves you with as little scarring as possible.
- All of us need to understand before death the *meaning* of our lives. What is your life all about?

Tools to Cope with the Fear of Death

Below are some recommendations for how you can prepare for your death or the death of a loved one. I've adapted them from the online article "How to Overcome Fear of Death."

1. Understand that death is a cycle. You are born, you die, and you are born again (depending on your spiritual beliefs). You're not being singled out.

2. Know that people won't forget you. You'll continue to be remembered on earth, and your memory will never disappear. Don't believe that as soon as you die, you'll disappear into oblivion.

3. Talk to someone you trust about your fear. See a therapist if your fear is extreme.

4. Don't worry until you need to. Learn to accept death as part of life. The average life span is seventy-five years in most developed countries, and you can still live a lot longer—a bonus!

5. Be optimistic. Studies show that optimists are less likely to contract heart disease than pessimists. If you have negative thoughts about the future, you're more likely to die sooner. So don't worry, and you'll live longer.

6. Death does not equal pain. Although life is a wonderful gift, remember that when you die, you'll not be in pain or suffering.

When my mother died at age seventy, I took her passing over very hard. I felt like a piece of my heart dropped away. I'm so grateful that Mom appears in my dreams—not as frequently as I'd like, but I still look forward to her appearances. She is a star in the night sky.

ACTIVITY 17

Plan Your End-of-Life Celebration

SUPPLIES: colored pens or markers, paper

When I was diagnosed with stage 4 colon cancer, I was advised to meet with an attorney to discuss my will. While I was at it, I also wrote my own obituary, so that task wouldn't become a burden for my loved ones. I felt so relieved when the work was completed. Next, I sat down to plan my end-of-life celebration.

I ASKED MYSELF THESE QUESTIONS:

1. Do I want a traditional funeral?
2. Do I want my remains to be buried or cremated?
3. How do I want my loved ones and friends to feel when I'm gone?
4. How do I want my life to be celebrated?
5. What needs to be included in the celebration?
6. What's the message I want to leave for loved ones and friends?
7. Who will make this celebration happen?

HERE'S MY PLAN:

1. No, I don't want a traditional funeral.
2. I prefer cremation.
3. I want my loved ones and friends to feel the love and joy I experienced in my life.
4. I want a PARTY!
5. My party will have music, food, cocktails, funny and poignant Alex stories, and a huge cake!
6. My message will be "NEVER GIVE UP!" Turn challenges into opportunities. Live each day with authenticity. Laugh—a lot! Love unconditionally.
7. All my loved ones and friends who want to be a part of this memorial.

Give yourself enough time and make sure you have the energy to answer the above questions.

HERE'S YOUR PLAN:

1.

2.

3.

4.

5.

6.

7.

Honor yourself and your life. You deserve it!

NEVER GIVE UP

6

Healing, Surviving, and Thriving

How You Can Survive and Thrive

Wow! I read over the previous chapters, and I'm glad I'm alive today. Still the question remains: How did I survive all these losses, traumas, and illnesses? What kept me fighting and overcoming?

Here's my answer:

Faith.	I believe in a Great Spirit and spiritual force.
Hope.	I believe in the greater good in life.
Love.	I believe in deep, unconditional love.
Power.	I believe I have the power to heal my mind, body, and spirit naturally in combination with my trusted health care professionals.
Drive.	I believe I have an inquisitive drive to understand and find answers about life.
Tools.	I believe in my tools for coping, surviving, and thriving.

What keeps you fighting and overcoming adversity? Respond to this question in the activity that follows.

ACTIVITY 18

Name Your Reasons for Fighting and Overcoming Adversity

Strength and Healing

In the previous chapter I discussed the tools that keep me thriving. The next six chapters focus on specific, powerful tools, which are the ingredients to live life to the fullest. If you work on developing these tools, you have the power to heal.

When life finds me at the end of my rope, I increase my prayers. When I pray, I pray for strength to manage my illnesses, strength to take on trauma, and strength to heal my life as fully as I can.

In 2007, I spent nearly sixty days in the hospital. When I was discharged, I couldn't walk. I had lost so much weight and muscle tone that my body couldn't stay upright. I eventually went from using a wheelchair to a walker, then a walker to a cane. I remember being totally out of breath when I returned home, but I was so proud of myself. Little by little, as my body healed, I grew stronger.

I didn't realize at first that as my body got stronger, so did my mind and spirit. The healing was fueled by the tiniest of successes, like remembering what day it was or being able to stay awake during conversations. As my physical strength grew, so did my emotional and spiritual strength. If I wanted to fully heal, I found the need to focus on all three.

Did I wait patiently for my strength and health to return? Of course not. I remember trying to go to a job interview after my first cancer surgery. I had lost thirty pounds and was still on pain medication, but here I was standing in the bathroom trying to get dressed. I was shaking so badly that I had to sit down on the edge of the bathtub. *I couldn't even get my pants on.*

I had a conversation with myself:

"What are you doing?" I asked myself.

"I'm getting ready for an interview," I replied.

"Alex," I said, "You've just been diagnosed with colon cancer and have had major surgery. Don't you think you should cancel the interview?"

"I can't," I replied to myself. "It's in two hours, and I've got to get a job."

My shoulders and hands shook violently. I started to sob.

Finally, after a ton of tears, I called and canceled the interview.

This was extremely difficult for me to do. I needed a job, and this position had a great salary and benefits package. I knew deep down, however, that I was in no shape to go to that interview. Pride and a keen sense of responsibility made me oblivious to the agony I was putting myself through. Finally, pain and common sense broke through, and I knew I needed to heal first.

It took all of my strength to pick up the phone and call the employer to explain that I could not continue with the interviews because I was fighting cancer. I didn't want sympathy; I just wanted to be honest with the employer—and with myself. I didn't have the strength to fight cancer and find a new job all at the same time.

I prayed for strength and healing to get me through all the surgeries, the difficulties of cancer, and the pain of unemployment.

Don't kid yourself—unemployment is traumatic. That sense of feeling worthless and unimportant is huge. If you're treated poorly and your job is eliminated, your self-image goes down the drain. The emotional part of me was so wounded. I was unemployed and had cancer. Talk about a double whammy.

When I was a child, I heard the priest at church say that God tests only the strong. I thought about that during those many nights in the hospital. Time after time, when I felt tested, I knew I was on my way to being the bionic woman. (Actually, with some of my parts gone, I do feel rather bionic!) Was I being tested to strengthen my ties to the Great Spirit? Or to prove that I'm a good person? Things in my life are never subtle. What I need to do is listen more carefully.

I discovered I made my own mistakes. My way of surviving trauma and loss was to get ill. Many times I tried to take the easy way out of a situation only to find there was no easy way. Luckily, I've learned that I don't have to get sick to get through trauma anymore. I can listen to my mind, body, and spirit to find out what it is I'm supposed to hear.

The next time you pray, pray for strength and healing.

ACTIVITY 19

Strengthen Your Memory

SUPPLIES: photo

This activity can be done while you're in the doctor's office or at the hospital, or in assisted living. It helps improve visual memory, attention, concentration, and recall abilities.

Choose a photo from your past. Focus on the photo for about one minute, memorizing as many details as possible. Turn over the photo so you can't see it, and list as many details from the photo as you can. Use the lines below.

How many details can you recall? What did you notice about the person or persons in the photo (clothing, expression, hairstyle, etc.), the setting, objects, and so forth?

Look at the photo again, and check to see how many details you recalled. Try the exercise again with a different photo. Exercises like this help improve your memory.

WHAT'S DIFFERENT BETWEEN THESE TWO PHOTOS?

The Healing Power of Gratitude

Thank you, Great Spirit, for everything.

The first time I took a vacation to Mexico, I was really surprised by what happened at sunset. People line up on the beach and by the pool to watch the sunset. Hundreds of people wait for the big golden ball to slide into the horizon. When it does, people start applauding. I've been to several places in western Mexico and Florida, and the same thing happens. People just gather to watch the sun set and applaud when it slowly sinks into the sea.

Imagine applauding the sun for setting with all its magnificent colors. Applauding an event that happens every day of the year. Applauding an event that's often taken for granted.

Now that's what I call gratitude.

I remember as a child looking out the back window in the kitchen and watching the sunset. In the winter on clear nights, the sky would turn several shades of red, and Mom would tell my siblings and me that Santa was making cookies. I loved that image, and I applauded in my little girl's heart.

Nature reminds me of gratitude. The sun, sky, power, calm, and wind. I don't need to be in Mexico to be filled with gratitude. The northern lights in a Minnesota night sky make me humble and amazed, too. I applaud it all.

Of all the wonders of the world, the greatest is gratitude.

Gratitude is a tool we can't keep to ourselves. It's a gift we give to others. When I was a child, my mother taught me to thank people for giving me gifts. I never understood the depth of this lesson until cancer struck. Somewhere deep down inside, I realized that I had a great deal to be grateful for and that I'd better start making sure that the Great Spirit, my family, and my friends knew how grateful I was. The line between life and death is thin. It's this thin line that matters most and increases my gratitude. I learned the hard way that I could lose everything I love in seconds.

I never go to sleep without thanking the Great Spirit for all that I've been given. Not a night goes by without the reminder of some gift I've been given during the day.

When my heart converges with my soul, I often feel this immense sense of gratitude. I get so darn sappy that you'd think I had too much to drink. But I don't need alcohol to feel grateful—I just need life.

Is it so hard for us to look at our friends and tell them flat out that we love them? Can we express our innermost gratitude to the people who have shaped our lives? Do we shy away from the emotions that come with gratitude? Is it because it's difficult to be vulnerable? Is it because the emotions are so strong, or is it the realization that our lives would be nothing without others?

While in the hospital, I was overwhelmed by the cards and flowers, phone calls and visits, and all the love and support I felt. I cried and cried often in the course of that first year with cancer. Every time I experienced a new challenge or setback, I was surrounded by friends and family who wanted nothing from me except for me to keep living. Within eleven months my CaringBridge site had over 12,500 hits. I got messages from people I haven't seen or heard from in years and from people I didn't even know. I was shocked that so many people were interested in my story and my healing.

In my awe, I remembered the first person who took an interest in my life and made me feel whole. She was my golf coach and home economics teacher in high school. I liked Miss B. the first time I met her. I wanted to be part of the girls' golf team. I wasn't the best golfer, but Miss B. saw my potential, and she worked with me. Every night after school, I was on either the golf course or an open field hitting golf balls. When the fall golf season ended, I continued to go to Miss B.'s classroom each night. We talked for hours. Okay, I talked for hours. She would listen to my stories about my life and would occasionally make a comment. It was so cathartic for me to tell her about my fears.

When the summer came and school was dismissed, I felt so alone without her. Then school would start again, and I would end up in her classroom every night. In retrospect, I'm embarrassed by the amount of time I spent in Miss B.'s classroom after school. I felt I couldn't let go of her. The night I graduated was one of the toughest of my life. I didn't know how I could survive without her.

Twenty years ago I sat down and wrote Miss B. a long overdue letter. I thanked her for all the time she spent with me. I explained how she made a difference in my life. I told her that I had been in a very vulnerable place in high school and that her support gave me the confidence to keep going. Yes, I told her in the letter that I had been abused by my father and that I was too ashamed to tell her back then. I apologized for all the times I screwed up on and off the golf course, and I asked that she forgive me.

Several years later, at my mother's funeral, Miss B. came in. She walked up the aisle in the church, and I saw her from one of the rooms in the back. I walked out into the aisle. When she saw me, we both broke into tears. She hadn't changed, but I had grown up. She told me she got my letter and thanked me for it. I shook my head and told her that it was I who was grateful for all that she'd done for me. The letter was only a means to let her know the amount of gratitude I had for her. When the funeral started, we said our good-byes.

I didn't think it would truly be our last good-bye.

One day, years later, my sister broke the news to me by email. In her message she had copied Miss B.'s obituary. I was stunned and heartbroken. I had so wanted to see Miss B. again, and now the opportunity was gone. Though I had thanked her in my letter years ago, I wanted to tell her in person that because of her, I never gave up nor would I ever give up. She was a wonderful mentor and friend, and I miss her dearly. I know her soul has gone on to a beautiful place, and I am comforted. I need to say, "Miss B., you saved my life, and I'm eternally grateful. Your presence in my life was a gift and one I will always cherish. I will remember you forever. Thank you."

What I've learned is that the Great Spirit sent Miss B. to help me survive growing up. And the Great Spirit continues to send me a lot of Miss B.'s to help me along the way.

I'd like to make a list of all my Miss B.'s, but to you it would just be a long list of names. The people on that list would be the ones who have helped me find the good in life and how to survive the bad. They've held my hand, they've let me cry on their shoulders, and they've given me hugs. They listened to my woes and helped me find some peace with their wisdom.

I owe my friends, family, and strangers a great deal of gratitude. Thank you for never giving up on me.

ACTIVITY 20

Show Gratitude

SUPPLIES: pen or pencil, greeting cards, stamps

Think of several recent, memorable occasions that warmed your heart or made you smile. Did someone say something to you or make you feel important? Did someone offer you a hug when no one else would? Did you laugh because of what someone said to you or did to you? Think about times when you felt loved, appreciated, or special.

Next, write these memories down so you can keep them with you forever.

PERSON/OCCASION	WHAT HAPPENED?	HOW DID YOU FEEL?
EXAMPLE:		
My "cancer-free" celebration	Over 80 people came to celebrate with me	Loved, happy, and joyous

Thank You

Now write a thank-you card and mail it, or tell the person (face to face or by phone) how they made you feel, think, or act.

Angels to the Rescue

As a child, I never understood why the angel on top of my family's Christmas tree leaned to the right. We tried hundreds of ways to "straighten" the angel, but she continued to list at the top of tree after tree, year after year. It was always the same. We'd gather around the tree to watch my mother place the angel on the top branch.

"Okay, close your eyes," she instructed, "and don't open them until I say."

A wooden chair scraped against the tiled floor. I could feel the heat from those old, large colored bulbs on my face. My youngest brother giggled. "Who's giggling?" My mother asked with her foot tapping on the chair. "Okay, you can open your eyes." A silence fell over us as we stood in brilliant suspension. In one collective breath, our excitement caused the tinsel to dance, sending waves of color throughout the room. My sister pointed her finger, her eyes wide and glued to the top of the tree. "Oh look, the angel is leaning *again*."

Our angel always leaned.

In response to our disappointment, my mother would bring the chair over and try to adjust the angel. She'd bend the branch back and forth or stuff more branches up the angel's white, lace skirt, but the results were always the same. Mom vowed for years to buy a new angel, but she never did.

By my fifth Christmas, I finally understood my family's situation—our angel reflected the devastating "elephant" in the midst of my family. We all leaned into my father's illness. Our wishes always included something to help him. Our love didn't seem enough.

On the eve of my thirty-fifth Christmas, I stood near the tree once again, looking up at the angel. This tree, however, belonged to my partner Rita's family, and we had gathered at her dad's to celebrate the holiday. Excited voices blinked loud and soft throughout the house, and laughter exploded in the kitchen.

I was looking at the Christmas tree when Rita asked me what I was staring at. I pointed to the angel on top of her father's tree. I asked her if he had ever had a problem with keeping his angel from leaning. She said no. I asked if he used anything special like wires or fishing line. She again said no. I raised my eyebrows. She walked away, shaking her head.

I turned toward the picture window. Snow was falling outside, and I could see the neighbor's nativity scene across the street. It was a picture-perfect Christmas Eve with all the trimmings: colored lights, delicious smells, and an angel that stood straight on top of the tree. I excused myself and went into the bathroom.

As a child I cried only in the bathroom. It was the one place in a home of nine kids and two adults where I could lock the door and let life's disappointments engulf me. I found that if I cried while splashing cold water on my face, I could reduce the red blotches and puffiness. Crying, to me, was a show of weakness. In the privacy of the pink-tiled walls and linoleum floor, I could let myself feel the despair.

In Rita's dad's house, I turned off the water in the guest bathroom and raised my head. Reflected in the oak mirror was the face of a little girl. The slightly crooked smile revealed a gap between her two front teeth, a dimple, and chubby cheeks. It was the dimple on the right cheek that made me recall a story my mother once told me when I was little.

"The moment before you were born, an angel came along and kissed you right here," Mom gently touched my right cheek. She tucked the blankets around me, bent down, kissed me on the forehead, and said, "This angel will watch over you and keep you safe."

In the sixty-watt light, I watched as the tears streamed down my face. I leaned against the wall. It never occurred to me to ask my mother what happens when angels fail. Now I have the knowledge that angels always succeed.

Every year for Christmas my mother received angels made out of wood, ceramic, porcelain, and pewter. Her greatest treasure, however, was her set of German-made, carved angels she began collecting as a young woman. Each of the fifty angels in the collection is two inches tall, and together they formed a miniature orchestra and choir. My two favorites consisted of an angel playing a black grand piano, while the other plucked the strings on a floor-length harp. At Christmas time, my mother would take them out and tell us the stories behind each piece—where she was when she got it, or who'd given the angel to her. As she spoke, a light would come into her eyes, and she would smile. I loved Mom's smile. I loved the gentle way she would place the angels back in their designated positions, putting them in almost military-like formation.

Now I, too, have a collection of angels, and I fully understand why my mother's belief in angels was so profound. As a child, and still to this day, I imagine that my angel looks like Mom. My angel is a cute little woman with big brown eyes, soft skin, and an animated smile.

I wonder what other survivors of child abuse think about their angels—that is, if they believe in angels at all. Everywhere I look

I see stories of how angels save lives. I read about them in magazines, see them on television and in movies, and hear about them on the radio. When angel stories are told, they end with some form of transformation.

When I graduated from college, I looked for a place to live in the Twin Cities. I met with the woman who owned an old house in south Minneapolis.

"Does your house have ghosts?" I asked her.

"No. What you'll find is a very nurturing and healing spirit in the house. People come here to heal," she said.

I was in the house for three months before a strange thing happened.

It was midnight, and I awoke feeling extremely lightheaded. I was sweating profusely. I heard someone call my name. When I looked up, there in the middle of my room stood a woman all in white with long black hair. I did not see her face.

"Get up and go to the kitchen. You need orange juice," she said.

I got up and went to the kitchen to get some juice to treat my insulin reaction and raise my blood sugar level. After I felt better, I got up, turned off the light, and left the kitchen.

As I was walking up the stairway to my bedroom, I heard the owner of the house call to me. I entered her room and sat on the edge of her bed.

Her eyes were wide. "You're not going to believe this, but a woman all in white with long black hair just woke me and told me you needed help. Are you okay?"

I nodded. "She was in my room and told me to get some orange juice. I had an insulin reaction, but I'm okay now." I stood to go back to my room, but before I left I asked the owner, "Who do you think that was?"

"Your spirit guide," she answered.

I'll remember that night for as long as I live. I am protected, and

I was protected all along. I didn't know it at the time, but I'm so blessed with this continual protection. Thank you, Great Spirit, and all the angels who protect me.

ACTIVITY 21

Develop Resiliency

SUPPLIES: pen or pencil

My son was around 3 years old. He was being taken care of by his Grandfather one day. Grandpa was outside working in the yard and had just dug a ditch. My son was very much into super heroes and often wore the pajamas that resembled super hero costumes all day long. This day however he didn't have the complete ensemble. He was being superman today and decided to "fly" over the ditch. As it happened he fell into the shallow ditch. When Grandpa lifted him out he exclaimed "I would have made it if I'd had my cape!"

—from KidSpirit's "Funny Kid Stories,"
kidspirit.com/stories.html

Notice how the little boy did *not* believe he had failed. He knew there was another way. We too often have a fear of failure, and it keeps us from trying.

If we trust in the Great Spirit, there is always a way. Our Great Spirit has infinite possibilities. If one way does not work, have faith that another way will be found. Great accomplishments come from great failures. We must be willing to pick ourselves up, dust ourselves off, and try again. Pick a new path or a different approach—put on a cape.

What ditch do you need to leap over?

Find your cape. Put it on. Feel confident.

Have faith that the universe will provide direction.

List your fear or what you need to overcome, your ditch. Write the quality to the left. On the right side, write one or two practical steps you can take to make it to the other side.

Examples:

QUALITY	DITCH	PRACTICAL STEPS
Trust	Healing from divorce	I'm dating again. I'm receiving many compliments. It feels great!
Faith	Healing from cancer	I had my last chemo session. I wrote a CaringBridge entry.

QUALITY	YOUR DITCH	PRACTICAL STEPS

I Believe in Hope

For a long time I wondered how to define "hope." One dictionary definition is "a feeling that what is wanted is likely to happen; desire accompanied by expectation." I want to say hope is more than a feeling, that it's a wish or a need, but every time I sit down to describe it, I use feeling statements. For example, "I wish I'd know how to deal with adversity." Underneath the words is a deeply felt need for hope.

Finding a definition perplexed me, so I thought if I can't define it, what if I used an image? I liked that idea. So I set off to find an image that worked for me. When the image came to me, I laughed. It was a lighthouse, the image I've had in my life all along. I have pictures and statues of lighthouses all over the house. I like how they stand tall and are so powerfully poised to take on the waves and nature's elements. I like the nautical theme of boats and lighthouses, so I started a collection. Lighthouses are my image of hope.

For years I was clinging to a sinking ship. I had no means of surviving the raging sea. I could only hold on to whatever piece of debris I could find. And then, out of the darkness, I saw a flash of light. I saw it again. I understood that if I could keep focused on the beacon, I could find my way to the shore. If I lost the light, I would lose my life. But the beacon continued to shine, and I was able to make it to the shore.

There is more than one storm in life. Looking back, I've had my share of turbulent seas and soul-raging waves. But I also know I was never meant to stay within the safety of the harbor. I've traveled and come upon amazing sights and sounds, like the northern lights on an autumn night in Wisconsin, sunsets in Acapulco, a full moon in Scotland, lightning flashes on Lake Superior, fresh volcanic ash on Mount St. Helens, and two rainbows at once. I've enjoyed the sight of a cardinal perched on the tree outside my window, a white-tailed doe lying down in the woods behind the house, my dog, Bob, going for his first swim in a lake, a newborn baby, and the love in my mother's eyes.

Think about what you've seen and heard in your life. Did you hope for someone to love or for a family? Did you hope for a house or a good job? Did you hope for spiritual guidance and comfort? Did you hope to live after a life-threatening illness or a horrible accident, or just for another breath of air, to walk again or survive unbearable pain? What would you have missed if you had stayed within the safety of the harbor?

I hoped the abuse would end—it did.

I hoped having diabetes wouldn't limit my life—it doesn't.

I hoped I would survive cancer—I did.

I hoped that I would be loved—I am.

I hoped to walk again and dance—I have.

I hoped to learn my purpose in life—I did.

I hoped to find meaning in my trauma—I did.

I hoped to forgive and love my dad—I do.

I hoped I'd make it through my dark moments—I did and continue to do so.

Having hope is like living a prayer. It's a source of comfort for me when things just don't seem right. Without hope, I could find no joy or pleasure in life. If I have something to hope for, I have something to live for.

> *The grand essentials of happiness are:*
> *something to do, something to love, and something to hope for.*
> **—Allan K. Chalmers**

This is my favorite quote on hope and I carry it with me. It motivates me to keep going, to keep living. I have something to do, someone to love, and something to hope for.

It's taken me a long time to write this chapter. So many wise people have described hope more eloquently than I. I can only tell you that having hope, for me, is much like taking a deep breath of air and then slowly releasing it. I have to hope. Things don't always turn out the way I planned, but now I see that hope is my lifeline. The abuse is over, but I know there will always be trauma, loss, and illness in the world. I remind myself daily that I can and will survive these events in my life because I have the tools within me.

I am a popcorn popper with all my hopes and dreams, beliefs and values, love and honor all flying around together. I will survive any trauma or loss that comes my way. My heart and soul are enlightened. My emotions are balanced and bring me joy. I know what profound love feels like. I have energy and a sound mind. I find joy in each day. My gratitude extends into the stars. I have hope, and I choose to never give up!

ACTIVITY 22

Write Your Bucket List of Hope

NEVER GIVE UP

SUPPLIES: pencil or pen or crayons and paper, or a computer

In the 2007 film *The Bucket List*, Jack Nicholson and Morgan Freeman play two terminally ill men who break out of a cancer ward and try to live their last days to the fullest.

Create a bucket list for the things you hope to do in your life.

Here's your bucket. Fill it.

Examples:

- Take a hot air balloon ride.
- Learn to ride a motorcycle.
- Travel to Europe, South America, or Antarctica.
- Learn to sing an opera.
- Help people who survive an earthquake, tsunami, or other disaster.
- Do your own routine at a comedy club.
- Write a book.
- Visit a place that has special meaning for you.
- Give donations to your favorite charities.
- Volunteer for a project you always wanted to do.
- Swim in an ocean or a lake.
- Take a class on a subject you always wanted to learn more about.
- Hold a baby.

Self-Inspiration to Get You Going

*When you know who you are; when your mission is clear
and you burn with the inner fire of unbreakable will; no cold can touch your heart;
no deluge can dampen your purpose. You know that you are alive.*

**—Chief Seattle, Duwamish tribe
(circa 1780–1866)**

If you're going through tough times right now—a divorce, loss of your home, a natural disaster, or the death of a loved one—where do you turn in this darkness? Where do you even start with finding your new normal?

My answer is to look for inspiration and self-inspiration.

Many dictionaries define inspiration as an act or quality that influences or arouses the mind, creative imagination, or emotions. Self-inspiration, therefore, is looking within your heart and soul to find the influences that motivate you to live a life of quality and to find happiness and joy. It's my belief that we've all felt a sense of inspiration at one time or another, such as a friend getting married, a new birth in the family, or a sunny day after days of rain and clouds.

There are so many different sources to inspire us:

- people and relationships
- the arts: music, theater, dance, poetry, books, painting, pottery, films
- nature
- animals
- weather
- spiritual beliefs
- quotes from mentors, teachers, and historical figures
- places

Self-inspiration may not be easy to find, since it involves going inside yourself, determining what your true potential is, and gaining insight on what moves and motivates you.

The key to self-inspiration is to find those things that can keep you from never giving up.

Our five senses include sight, smell, taste, touch, and hearing. Our sixth sense involves our intuition, our awareness of otherworldliness, and our belief in a higher being. We have different names for this eternal energy, but, no matter what we name it, there is comfort and motivation from this supreme source.

In Chapter 1, I mentioned how I love Higher Brain Living. After each session, I find myself in awe of all the opportunities I have in this life. I feel pure joy and motivation to reach beyond my limits. I am confident and unstoppable, even though I may be going through a difficult time. I don't let stress or illness block my way from feeling loved and supported.

Tools for Inspiration

There are so many places in our world where we can let the spirit move us. Sometimes all we need to do is go deep inside of ourselves to find inspiration. These tools can also help.

1. Pets. My dog, Bob, is one of my favorite inspirations. No matter how bad a day is, he's waiting at the door, wagging his tail. How can I not smile the moment I meet his eyes? Pets have a wonderful way of inspiring us. If you don't have a dog or cat, visit the Humane Society, and ask to play with or hold an animal. They love the attention. There's nothing like a cat purring in your arms.

2. Travel. One of my favorite inspirations is traveling, and you can make it one of yours. Visiting the Grand Canyon may astound you and add some awesomeness in your life. Are there places you'd like to explore? How about Irish or Scottish castles, the Swiss Alps, or a sunset in Mexico? There are so many unique places to visit here on Earth. All you have to do is make a list of spots you'd love to visit, save money for your trip, and let the sights fuel your spirit. I make this sound so easy, but it takes planning and perseverance. For most of us traveling is expensive. Start a savings account for traveling, and put deposits into it each month. If you can't travel due to financial or personal reasons, try exploring other countries through films, art exhibits, community education classes, or friends' photos.

3. Outdoors. If world traveling isn't an option, try going to different places in your state. There are lakes, mountains, seashores, forests, gardens, state parks, and so many other places to see. Look for tourist adventures in your state. Check out your local parks or other outdoor attractions you haven't experienced. Start dreaming, and make it happen.

4. Passion. I'm passionate about volunteering, golfing, and adventure. These passions inspire me. Anything you love to do and do often is a passion and inspiration, too. When you volunteer you can get a "helper's high." By helping others, you help yourself. Do you have passion for a cause, activity, or adventure? What makes your heart beat faster? Take a look at Exercise 3, "Things I Like to Do List," at the end of this book. This exercise will help you hone in on your passions.

5. Silence. Yes, silence is inspiring. In a state of silence, you find rest and relaxation. It's a time of peace, acceptance, and passion. Open your ears and your heart to the messages from the universe. What are you hearing? Is there a theme? Meditation is a great way to condition yourself to be comfortable with silence. Try having quiet time each day to be alone, thoughtful, and reflective. Finding silence in our society is never easy, but the rewards, such as increased energy, deep concentration in meditation, outward activity, and inner serenity, are worth it.

ACTIVITY 23

Create Your Inspiration Wall

SUPPLIES: camera, computer and printer or magazines, paper, scissors, glue or tape

Sometimes you look at a photo and exclaim, "I love this!" You feel inspired by the image. Spend some time looking through magazines or online, and find those pictures that make you say "Wow!" You can also choose your own personal photos. Include only the photos that inspire you. Then start creating your Inspiration Wall—a collage of inspirational images.

When you see a photo that immediately makes your heart beat faster, make a copy for your Inspiration Wall. Keep these images close at hand. They can lift you up.

To me, these images say "inspiration."

Don't Forget Forgiveness

You've probably wondered why I haven't listed "forgiveness" as a tool. I've had problems with forgiveness. I learned the hard way that forgiveness and letting go are great tools to have in my tool kit. You can imagine with all of the abuse, loss, and illness, forgiveness was difficult for me to absorb. My biggest problem was that I didn't know where to start, so I decided to do some research.

I read books and attended forgiveness classes. I tried to work diligently on forgiving others. I kept looking for the key to forgiveness. I found it in one of my classes when we went through a forgiveness meditation. Tears started rolling down my face when the facilitator asked, "Do you forgive yourself?"

WHAM!

I almost toppled over. This was such an alien question, and it hit me hard. "Do I forgive myself?" An "aha" moment occurred. As a frightened child, a troubled teenager, and an angry adult, I couldn't see how I could forgive myself for all the dramatics I caused. Then I remembered my inner child, who was still so hurt and afraid. She deserved to be forgiven, didn't she? This is where I needed to start—this was the key.

Forgiving yourself and others is difficult but attainable. For two years I learned a lot about forgiveness—what it was and whom it's for. I wasn't surprised to find out that forgiveness is a two-way street. Everyone on the freeway of life needs to forgive and be forgiven. First I had to forgive myself before I forgave others. I knew forgiving my dad would be HUGE!

In my research I found that there is no place in the Bible that states, "Forgive and forget." The Bible also doesn't say anything about forgiving yourself. From Luke 6:37 we learn: "Do not judge and you will not be judged. Do not condemn, and you will not be condemned. Forgive, and you will be forgiven." Then there's the Lord's Prayer, which in one version says, "Forgive us our debts as we forgive our debtors."

Since the phrase "forgive and forget" didn't come from the Bible, where did it come from? It actually appeared in the work of two early European writers. Miguel de Cervantes (1547–1616) wrote, "Let us forgive and forget injuries," while William Shakespeare (1564–1616) wrote, "Pray you now, forget and forgive."

Forgiveness doesn't come easy for most of us. Our instincts are to recoil in self-protection when we've been physically and emotionally injured. We don't naturally overflow with mercy, grace, and forgiveness when we've been hurt. But when we refuse to forgive someone, it doesn't make the pain go away—we just continue to hurt ourselves.

Forgiveness is a choice. Forgiveness is not forgetting about an offense, but rather choosing to overlook the wrong you have suffered and releasing the anger and bitterness it caused. To forgive does not mean you condone harmful behavior. Forgiveness actually creates space in your heart and mind that must be soft and open to forgive. Freeing someone of the pain they caused you gives your heart room to feel peace, joy, and true happiness. According to the article "The Benefits of Forgiveness," Dr. Fred Luskin, director of the Stanford Forgiveness Project, points to research showing that holding grudges leads to "long-term damage to the cardiovascular system," while forgiveness boosts one's immune system as well as lowering stress and improving self-confidence.

In the book *The Language of Recovery* Gerald Jampolsky writes, "Forgiveness can be the emotional glue that puts brokenness back together."

Here are some of my favorite quotations about forgiveness:

> *Forgiveness is to set a prisoner free, and to realize the prisoner [is] you.*
> **—Corrie Ten Boom, a Christian woman who survived a Nazi concentration camp during the Holocaust**

> *[Forgiveness is] to accept the fact that the past can't change.*
> **—Oprah Winfrey**

> *I think one should forgive and remember. . . . If you forgive and forget in the usual sense, you're just driving what you remember into the subconscious; it stays there and festers. But to look, even regularly, upon what you remember and know you've forgiven is an achievement. Remembering doesn't mean recreating the pain. The pain is toxic. Remembering makes us sensitive to similar situations of hurt. It provides us with a chance to react differently—in a more forgiving, loving way.*
> **—Faith Baldwin,** ***The West Wind***

Forgiving My Father and More

I went to a meeting one night at a coffee shop. I ordered a latte but forgot to ask for decaf rather than regular. (I can't do caffeine; it gives me migraines and insomnia.) Whoa, I was flying. When I got home and went to bed, I couldn't sleep, so I decided to practice forgiveness. I took several deep breaths and exhaled slowly. When I was ready, I started with myself. I spent two hours acknowledging the times I was wrong. When I truly felt I could forgive myself, I took some more deep breaths. I then concentrated on forgiving my dad.

I spent four hours in an honest conversation with him in my head. I told him that he had hurt me deeply and shared with him my memories of abuse and betrayal. I asked him why he denied getting help for himself. Why did he hurt everyone he knew? Why was he so angry and mean? The questions just poured out of my heart. I would never know the answers. When I finally let go of my anger and hurt, I was exhausted (but not sleepy). Finally, I said to Dad, "I forgive you for all the pain, anger, and hurt you caused me, whether you did it intentionally or unintentionally." Then I turned it around and asked for his forgiveness. At the end of our conversation I felt as if ten tons of weight had fallen off my body. I was feeling peaceful and calm. I forgave him.

I began to forgive others I had hurt and those who had hurt me. I was very direct and authentic. It took me six hours, and when I was done, I fell asleep. The next day I felt free.

Forgiving is not easy, but it needs to be done. You and I have to work daily on forgiving ourselves and others. If we don't, pain and hurt will increase in weight as the years go by. That weight will weaken your immune system, and you're at greater risk of becoming ill. I learned the hard way. Now I know better, and my immune system has become healthier. How do I know this? Because I feel hopeful, and I can laugh again. I've realized that when I remember some horrible hurt, I need to take a couple of deep breaths, slow my breathing, and remind my mind-body-spirit that I can forgive—myself and others.

Tools to Learn How to Forgive

Ill will, grudges, and resentments make us physically and emotionally sick by lowering our immune system. These tools can help you move beyond resentment and toward forgiveness.

1. Acknowledge that you've been hurt. Be honest and objective in looking at the part you played in the situation.

2. Remember that no matter how hard you try to be perfect, you are human, and humans make mistakes.

3. Forgive yourself first. If you can't, chances are good that you won't be able to forgive others.

4. Make room for love. It's difficult for love to live in your heart when you are angry and resentful.

5. It takes energy to hang on to anger, hurt, and betrayal. When you are hurt, you need all your energy to heal your mind, body, and spirit.

If forgiveness remains an obstacle, seek professional help to learn how to open your heart, survive the harm, and forgive.

ACTIVITY 24

Practice Forgiveness and Letting Go

SUPPLIES: pen or pencil, paper,
weights or dumbbells, box, match or lighter

Write down resentments that you still carry around in your heart. Keep it brief, but get your feelings out. How did you feel when this happened to you? Does it still hurt when you think about the loss, trauma, or illness? Fold the piece of paper in half, and hold it in your hand.

Select a weight or dumbbell that represents the weight or seriousness of the hurt you still feel in your heart. Pick it up. Select one and place it in a box.

Notice how the box fills up with weights—the hurts and resentments that you carry around in your heart. See how the box gets heavier and heavier. Try to lift the box. How heavy does it feel? How heavy is your hurt?

The box represents your heart and the burdens you carry around inside every single day. Forgiveness and letting go are the keys to a lighter, freer, happier heart and to wellness. Forgiveness is challenging and difficult. But we forgive so we can  heal. We release the resentment so we can be happier and healthier.

Now take your folded piece of paper with your hurt/resentment on it, and step outside. Visualize letting go of this pain forever. Set the paper on fire with a match or lighter.

You may need to do this forgiveness exercise a number of times before the pain is completely released. Be gentle with yourself. You're cleansing and healing your spirit. It may take a number of repetitions. You'll know when you are healed—when you no longer feel any resistance to forgiving someone.

Life Passion

*There are passions far more exciting than the physical ones
[such as] intellectual passion, mathematical passion,
passion for discovery and exploration: the mightiest of all passions.*
—**George Bernard Shaw**

Passion is pure energy, much like putting a spark to wood chips in a bonfire. It engulfs us so that we may become the most authentic people we can be. Passion is the fuel we need to ignite our lives and dreams. The Great Spirit gave us passion when we were born—one of our natural gifts. Our hopes and desires fuel this energy. Each of us possess this powerful energy—and the ability to keep it burning.

How do you consciously and consistently bring more of yourself into what you do? One simple approach is to go beyond identifying what you love and ask yourself why you love it. Do some reverse engineering to identify the underlying characteristics that tend to be in place when you're feeling passionate.

If you look close enough, you'll find your passion in your wishes and dreams. When friends kept encouraging me to write my story, the idea (which was already in my heart) began to slowly form in my brain. The task seemed all-consuming, but I found the passion I needed to share this story with you.

Tools for Finding Your Passion

Here are some tools to try if you're seeking your passion.

1. State your intention. In this way you will clarify for yourself what you desire. Intentions let the Universe know that what you desire is for the greater good of yourself and others.

2. Push past your fear. Your comfort zone may be holding you back from experiencing true passion. Do you remember the dreams you had when you were a child? What fear kept you from achieving these dreams? Is the fear due to feelings of being not good enough, not creative enough, or not trusting yourself? Write what the fear is on a blank piece of paper, then add words that accompany this fear. When you're done, flip the paper over, and start to list all the things you'd like to try—activities that bring you joy and make you feel confident. Start out small so you don't come up against a sense of failure.

3. Find passion in your heart rather than relying on your mind. Thinking about your passion is difficult—you have to get your heart involved. What do you do that makes your heart sing? I have a passion for fishing. My joy and happiness come when I just sit in the boat and enjoy the outdoors. This is heaven to me whether I catch a fish or not.

4. Take action to find passion. You have to try out many things before you can identify your passion. If you try something and it doesn't do anything for you at first, make a second or third attempt. Some passions take time to cultivate before they ignite. Keep your heart and spirit fueled with passion, and life will show you some amazing things.

ACTIVITY 25

Finish the Sentence
"I Love Myself Because . . ."

SUPPLIES: colored pens or markers, paper

Have you ever asked yourself why you love something? Most of us know what and who we love but never go deep enough to understand why we love something or someone. Why do you love your partner? Why do you love your pet? Why do you love your house or neighborhood? Now for the biggest Why question of all: Why do you love yourself? Do you have an answer? If not, the diagram below will help you define the reasons you love yourself.

Write words or draw objects that make you feel alive and loved. Finish the sentence: *I love myself because . . .*

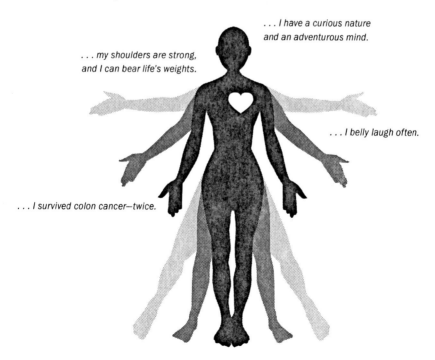

. . . I have a curious nature and an adventurous mind.

. . . my shoulders are strong, and I can bear life's weights.

. . . I belly laugh often.

. . . I survived colon cancer—twice.

NEVER GIVE UP

7

Putting Your New Life Together

What It All Means

One benefit of trauma and loss is that we have the right to take whatever meaning we want from them. I could look back over my life and think, "Wow, my life sucks." But I don't believe this because, in the midst of trauma and loss, I found moments of incredible wonder, like those breathtaking moments when everything makes sense and reveals a purpose. Moments when you feel nothing but pure love and absolute joy. I have found sublime happiness.

For some reason I didn't die in the car accident. For other reasons I didn't die from colon cancer or ARDS. So what am I to make of this? I found the meaning of things I cannot live without—joy, love, prayer, and laughter—and some of the tools I discussed in this book. I need to live fully and experience love in my life. I need my tools to go forward.

In remission, I suddenly realized that I wasn't the same woman I was before my cancer diagnosis. Things had changed, and I had changed. How was I supposed to exist in this new perspective—in this new normal? How was I supposed to live? Then I took the Renewing Life course. It's described as a process that helps you make meaning, grow from illness, and become empowered as you build coping and communication skills.

To my amazement, not only did Renewing Life change my life, it saved my life. In the second week, we focused on the healing partnership of mind, body, and spirit. I was immediately captured by a quote from a person with AIDS: "When one is faced by one's mortality, one has to reevaluate how one is going to live." I dug in and identified the things that no longer work for me and opened myself up to different skills that could bring more joy and passion into my life. Living authentically aligns your body, mind, and spirit with your heart and fills your actions with powerful life-force energy. I found that using this life-force energy enhanced my healing, because I am my physician within.

Through readings and activities I can look myself in the mirror and say, "I love you, Alex," and I mean it. My core consists of deep love and compassion. I learned that I wasn't a bad person after all. The traumas, losses, and illnesses I've experienced were ways I learned compassion, forgiveness, and how to love myself.

I'm not the monster I thought I was.

I'm making my life full of meaning and purpose by reminding myself to be real, to always be authentic with my emotions, and to express them in appropriate ways. I *can* keep my immune system healthy. My health means everything to me, and through my illnesses, traumas, and losses I have learned that there's a better way for me to live. These experiences have taught me to love and trust myself, be grateful for all that I have in my life, and love and forgive unconditionally.

I encourage you to find the authentic you. When you do, you'll find the true meaning in every experience, whether it's traumatic or not. You'll have the power to create the life you've always wanted.

Your tool kit to cope with stress, trauma, loss, and illness has always been within you. The exercises at the end of the book are your maps to your specific tools. Keep a list in your purse or wallet as a reminder when stress, trauma, loss, or illness occurs. Using your tools can increase the quality of your life.

ACTIVITY 26

Turn Old Thoughts into New Thoughts

SUPPLIES: pen or pencil and paper

We've all heard the term "dirty laundry." I'm not asking you to air out all your dirty laundry—your secrets. Doing laundry is a maintenance activity. Some of us do body-mind-spirit laundry many times per week (no suds needed).

Think of this activity as a regular, maintenance cleansing of your mind. Do you have some weekly thoughts that are muddy, smelly, or soiled in some manner?

Let's clean them up. You'll turn your old, negative thoughts into something more hopeful and positive.

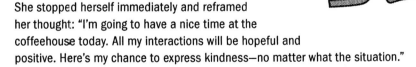

For example: One day my friend Shelly found herself thinking, "Oh no! That jerky guy is at my coffeehouse again. There's his car. How am I going to avoid him this time? Wow, he bugs me!"

She stopped herself immediately and reframed her thought: "I'm going to have a nice time at the coffeehouse today. All my interactions will be hopeful and positive. Here's my chance to express kindness—no matter what the situation."

The jerky guy ended up becoming her friend. Shelly found out the man had lost his wife less than two years earlier. As Shelly opened herself to love rather than fear, her relationship with this man, as well as others, improved. The judging part of Shelly lessened, and the loving, accepting part of her increased.

Write down a negative, fear-based statement you made today or in the past week, and then reframe this thought with a more intentionally positive outcome.

What I Learned from Cancer

A diagnosis of cancer doesn't mean a death sentence.
Cancer is a wake-up call.
Your attitude is more indicative of your prognosis than
    a blood test.
Talk honestly about your emotions to strengthen your
    immune system.
Express your anger in healthy ways.
Serious and life-threatening illnesses are times of personal
    transformation.
Being positive in the midst of a crisis is very difficult,
    but do it anyway.
A wonderful life means being and accepting who you are—
    good and bad.
Practice resilience to help you bounce back from life's woes.
Pay attention to pain—it's the body's way of crying for help.
Breathe deeply, and give yourself additional energy
    to face difficulties.
Nourishing people accompany you on your journey,
    while toxic people drain your energy.
There will be days when all you can do is cry, breathe,
    and survive.

Your loved ones cannot fix you.
Love yourself unconditionally—self-love is the foundation of your being.
Negative feelings weaken your immunity.
Recognize your need for time-outs—it's better than a major burnout.
Crying is giving your soul a voice, but crying all the time will give you a headache.
Develop friendships that make you feel inspired.
Laughing relieves stress and sometimes the bladder.

8

Fine-Tuning Your Tools

Your Most Valuable Tools

Each of us possesses tools to survive the ups and downs of life. Your tool kit is filled with tangible and intangible ways of coping. You may or may not be aware of your tools on a conscious level, but they are nestled inside of you and emerge when you experience stress, trauma, loss, or illness.

These tools can help you to survive, thrive, and energize.

Complete each exercise that follows, and in the last exercise you'll list all of your coping tools. This is your personal tool kit. You can add more tools as you want. There is an endless array of tools to bring quality into your daily life.

You can survive and thrive!

EXERCISE 1

Life Stress Test

Which of the major life events listed in the table below have taken place in your life in the past twelve to twenty-four months?

Mark down the points for each event that you have experienced this year.

When you're done looking at the whole list, add up the points for each event. Then check your life stress score on the next page.

POINTS	EVENTS
100	Death of a spouse/partner
73	Divorce
65	Marital separation or separation from relationship partner
63	Jail Term
63	Death of close family member
50	Marriage
47	Fired from work
45	Marital reconciliation
45	Retirement
44	Change in family member's health
40	Pregnancy
39	Sex difficulties
39	Addition to family
39	Business readjustment
38	Change in financial status
37	Death of close friend
36	Change to a different line of work
35	Change in number of marital arguments
31	Mortgage or loan over $30,000
30	Foreclosure of mortgage or loan
29	Change in work responsibilities
29	Trouble with in-laws
28	Outstanding personal achievement

POINTS	EVENTS
26	Spouse begins or stops work
26	Starting or finishing school
25	Change in living conditions
24	Revision of personal habits
23	Trouble with boss
20	Change in work hours, conditions
20	Change in residence
20	Change in schools
19	Change in recreational habits
19	Change in church activities
18	Change in social activities
17	Mortgage or loan under $20,000
16	Change in sleeping habits
15	Change in number of family gatherings
15	Change in eating habits
13	Vacation
12	Holiday season
11	Minor violations of the law
_____	**Your Total Score**

This exercise is adapted from Dr. Tim Lowenstein's 2011 "Life Stress Test" (http://www.cliving.org/lifestresstest.htm). It is used with permission.

This scale shows the kind of life pressure that you are facing. Depending on your coping skils or the lack thereof, this scale can predict the likelihood that you will fall victim to a stress-related illness. The illness could be mild—frequent tension headaches, acid indigestion, loss of sleep—to very serious illness like ulcers, cancer, migraines, and the like.

Life Stress Scores

0-149: Low susceptibility to stress-related illness

150-299: Medium susceptibility to stress-related illness. Learn and practice relaxation and stress management skills and a healthy lifestyle.

300 and over: High susceptibility to stress-related illness. Daily practice of relaxation skills is important for your wellness. Take care of it now, before a serious illness erupts or an affliction becomes worse.

EXERCISE 2

When I . . .

Complete the following list of unfinished questions with action verbs (such as *laugh*, *take a walk*, *cry*). Each question may have several answers. After you finish, go back and circle or highlight the action verbs you used.

For example:
When I get angry, I (express) my emotions clearly so I don't harm myself or others.
When I get angry, I (ask) questions to help me understand the issue.

Now your turn:
When I am disappointed, I _____

When I need to relax, I _____

When I'm feeling peaceful, I _____

When someone hurts me, I _____

When I need to tell someone about my feelings, I _____

When I'm stressed, I _____

When I need comfort or support, I _____

When I listen to music, I _____

When I get irritated by a loved one, I _____

When I'm confronted on something I've said or done, I _____

When I lose, I _____

When I win, _____

When I have extra time, I _____

When I'm in an accident, I _____

When I experience a trauma or loss, I _____

When I feel like giving up, I _____

When I am bored, I _____

When I am afraid, I _____

When I feel rejected and abandoned, I _____

When I feel depressed or anxious, I _____

When I have difficulty sleeping, I _____

When I feel out of control, I _____

When I am tired, I _____

When I am in pain, I _____

List your action verbs here:

EXERCISE 3

Things I Like to Do

Things you like to do are often activities that strengthen your immune system. Check the activities below that you feel help you cope with trauma, loss, or intense situations. Add others that are not listed here.

✓	ACTIVITY	✓	ACTIVITY
	Spend time sitting by a lake		Teach a hobby
	Listen to music		Babysit
	Take a walk with a friend		Garden, pull weeds, or landscape
	Take a walk alone		Learn a new language
	Exercise		Bike
	Read		Take photographs of nature
	Write in a journal		Stargaze
	Go camping		Go antiquing
	Talk on the phone with a friend		Clean the house
	Cook or bake		Host a dinner party
	Laugh		Sit in the sunshine
	See a movie or watch a DVD		Visit a long-distance friend
	Knit, sew, or crochet		Build something
	Fix cars		Draw, paint, or make pottery
	Go online		Volunteer
	Swim, hike, golf, or climb		Play a board game
	Sing or write music		Take up judo, tai chi, or qigong
	Meditate, pray, or visualize		Study feng shui
	Go to a spa		Dance
	Attend a concert or play		Join a book club
	Travel		Take a nap
	Take a class		Go to a sporting event

EXERCISE 4

Your Tools

Review Exercises 2 and 3. Write down what tools you have and describe how each tool helps you cope. When you've finished, copy this list, and tape it to a mirror in your home or the dashboard of your car. When you need a tool to deal with a situation, look at the list, and pick the tool that will help you the most.

HERE IS MY LIST, TO HELP YOU IDENTIFY YOURS

Speak honesty	Be optimistic
Go to therapy	Take care of myself
Write	Accept/Anticipate change
Use humor	Make goals
Be resilient	Take action
Express anger	Learn new things
Pray	Maintain perspective
Go to a self-defense class	Believe in angels
Play music	Consult medical specialists
Read	Learn from my experiences
Relocate	Find meaning
Wear safety goggles	Love
Exercise	Take medication as prescribed
Meditate	Eat healthy foods
Take antidepressants as prescribed	Sleep/nap
Breathe deeply	Listen to guided meditations
Talk	Talk to friends
Listen	Express gratitude
Walk with Bob	Find strength
Sit by Lake Superior or in nature	Get connected
Be quiet	Hope
Apply ice	Be inspired
Find insurance	Watch for mini-miracles
Eat right	Sing
Change my attitude	Play
See my health care team	Bake/cook
Use life-affirming messages	Drink plenty of water

THIS IS YOUR TOOL KIT. CONGRATULATIONS!

1.
2.
3.
4.
5.
6.
7.
8.
9.
10.
11.
12.
13.
14.
15.
16.
17.
18.
19.
20.
21.
22.
23.
24.
25.
26.
27.
28.
29.
30.
31.
32.
33.
34.
35.
36.
37.
38.
39.
40.
41.
42.
43.
44.
45.
46.
47.
48.
49.
50.

Resources

American Cancer Society
www.cancer.org
Provides information, referrals, and research funding; sponsors major fundraisers and awareness activities; lobbies local and national government officials; has offices around the country.
250 Williams St. NW, Atlanta, GA 30303
(800) 227-2345

Angel Foundation
www.mnangel.org
Provides emergency financial assistance, education, and support to adults living with cancer and their families.
700 S 3rd St., Suite 106W, Minneapolis, MN 55415
(612) 627-9000

Pathways: Health Crisis Resource Center
www.pathwaysminneapolis.org/
Provides classes, special events, and individual sessions on holistic health. I particularly recommend the Renewing Life program, with support groups and educational programs offering a variety of healing techniques.

3115 Hennepin Ave. S, Minneapolis, MN 55408
(612) 822-9061

Regions Hospital Cancer Care Center
www.regionshospital.com/cancer
Provides oncology consults, hematology consults, bleeding clotting consults, bone marrow biopsies, chemotherapy infusions, blood product administration, genetic counseling, and a survivorship program.
640 Jackson St., St. Paul, MN 55101
(651) 254-3572

Well Within: A Nonprofit Holistic Wellness Resource Center
www.wellwithin.org
Connects health care consumers and caregivers with local resources that specialize in integrated or complementary medicine, as well as other resources for getting healthy and staying well. Also offers the Renewing Life program.
1811 Weir Dr., Suite 230, Woodbury, MN 55125
(651) 451-3113

Sources Cited

1. CAUTION: Stress Is Extremely Dangerous

Lutz, Ashley. "18 Terrifying Facts about How Stress Can Totally Destroy Your Body." *Business Insider*, June 11, 2012. http://www.businessinsider.com/facts-about-stress-and-your-health-2012-6.

"Stress Is Just as Catching as the Flu." *Star Tribune* (Minneapolis), January 12, 2014.

"What Is HBL?" Higher Brain Living. http://www.higherbrainliving.com/what-is-hbl. Accessed March 11, 2014.

2. The Nasty and Nurturing Sides of Anger

Prosser, Courtney. "Is Suppressed Anger Making You Sick?" *MindBodyGreen*, July 3, 2013. http://www.mindbodygreen.com/0-10153/is-suppressed-anger-making-you-sick.html.

3. The Mind-Body-Spirit Connection in Healing

Conway, Chris. "The Attitude of Survival." *Backcountry Attitude*. http://www.backcountryattitude.com/survival_attitude.html. Accessed March 4, 2014.

Hyatt, Pam, and Caroline White. "Consequences of Child Sexual Abuse in a Woman's Life: A Case Study." School of Social Work, College of St. Catherine and the University of St. Thomas, 2007.

Porter, James. "Fight, Flight or Freeze Response to Stress." *Stress Stop*, June 12, 2012. http://stressstop.com/stress-tips/articles/fight-flight-or-freeze-response-to-stress.php.

Sternberg, Esther M., and Philip W. Gold. "The Mind-Body Interaction in Disease." *Scientific American*, March 17, 2002.

4. The Truth About Childhood Sexual Abuse

Browne, Angela, and David Finkelhor. "Impact of Child Sexual Abuse: A Review of the Research." *Psychological Bulletin* 99, no. 1 (1986): 66–77.

"Child Maltreatment 2009." U.S. Department of Health and Human Services, Administration for Children and Families, Administration on Children, Youth and Families, Children's Bureau, 2010. http://www.acf.hhs.gov/programs/cb/stats_research/index.htm#can.

Devlin, Kieron. "Writing as Healing: A Pen Is Mightier Than a Pill." http://www.kierondevlin.com/free-articles/free-articles_3_a-pen-is-mightier-than-a-pill.htm. Accessed March 4, 2014.

"The Facts on Children and Domestic Violence." Futures Without Violence, 2008. http://www.futureswithoutviolence.org.

Hay, Louise L. *Heal Your Body: The Mental Causes for Physical Illness and the Metaphysical Way to Overcome Them*. Carlsbad, CA: Hay House, 1987.

McGee, Joe. "Laughing Is No Laughing Matter." *Patriot Ledger*, June 12, 2002. http://www.laughterforhealth.com/press_room.html.

6. The Nightmare of Sexual Exploitation

Bailey, Covert, and Lea Bishop. "Can Exercise Make Me High?" *Health Central*, September 17, 2001. http://www.healthcentral.com/fitorfat/408/41285.html.

Jorgenson, Linda Mabus. "Countertransference and Special Concerns of Subsequent Treating Therapists of Patients Sexually Exploited by a Previous Therapist." TELL: Therapy Exploitation Link Line, 1995. http://www.therapyabuse.org/p2-inappropriate-countertransference.htm.

Khalsa, Dharma Singh, and Cameron Stauth. *Meditation as Medicine: Activate the Power of Your Natural Healing Force*. New York: Simon & Schuster, 2001.

7. Osteoarthritis Defense

"The Basics of Osteoarthritis." Osteoarthritis Health Center, WebMD. http://www.webmd.com/osteoarthritis/guide/osteoarthritis-basics. Accessed March 6, 2014.

"What Is Qigong?" Tiantian Qigong. http://www.tiantianqigong.com/whatis.html. Accessed March 4, 2014.

9. Illness as Trauma

Naparstek, Belleruth. *Invisible Heroes: Survivors of Trauma and How They Heal*. New York: Bantam Books, 2004.

O'Neil, Dennis. "Explanations of Illness." Medical Anthropology: How Illness Is Traditionally Perceived and Cured Around the World. July 12, 2006. anthro.palomar.edu/medical/med_1.htm.

11. Sleep Apnea: When You Can't Breathe When You Sleep

"Consequences of Insufficient Sleep." Healthy Sleep. Division of Sleep Medicine, Harvard Medical School. 2008. http://healthysleep.med.harvard.edu/healthy/matters/consequences.

"Sleep Apnea." American Sleep Apnea Association. 2013. http://www.sleepapnea.org/learn/sleep-apnea.html.

12. Cancer: A Life Changer

"Acute Respiratory Distress Syndrome." MedlinePlus. US National Library of Medicine, National Institutes of Health. March 3, 2012. http://www.nlm.nih.gov/medlineplus/ency/article/000103.htm.

Bosniak, Kanta. *Surviving Cancer: A Sacred Journey: Guided Imagery for Women*. Audiobook CD. Wernersville, PA: Kanta Bosniak, 2008.

"Minneapolis Neuromuscular Therapy." Benessere: Body in Balance. 2013. http://www.benesserebodyinbalance.com/NEUROMUSCULAR_THERAPY.htm.

Naparstek, Belleruth. *Invisible Heroes: Survivors of Trauma and How They Heal*. New York: Bantam Books, 2004.

13. Your New Normal

Renewing Life Within, Renewing Life Together. Facilitators' Manual. Minneapolis: Pathways, 2013.

14. Setbacks in Healing

"CyberKnife FAQs." PeaceHealth Southwest Medical Center. http://www.peacehealth.org/southwest/services/cyberknife-center/Pages/cyberknife-faqs.aspx. Accessed March 6, 2014.

17. How to Talk with Your Dying Loved Ones

LeShan, Lawrence. *Cancer as a Turning Point: A Handbook for People with Cancer, Their Families, and Health Professionals*. Revised edition. New York: Plume, 1994.

Volt, Zoe, Mr Stephen, et al. "How to Overcome Fear of Death." http://www.wikihow.com/Overcome-Fear-of-Death. Accessed March 6, 2014.

22. I Believe in Hope

Webster's New World College Dictionary. 4th edition. Cleveland: Wiley, 2007.

24. Don't Forget Forgiveness

Duenwald, Mary. "The Benefits of Forgiveness." *Ladies' Home Journal*. http://www.lhj.com/health/stress/relaxation-techniques/the-benefits-of-forgiveness. Accessed March 6, 2014.

The Language of Recovery—and Living Life One Day at a Time: A Blue Mountain Arts Collection. Boulder: Blue Mountain Press, 2000.